# Herbal Remedies

# Herbal Remedies

*A Practical Beginner's Guide to Making
Effective Remedies in the Kitchen*

## Christopher Hedley

## Non Shaw

First published in Great Britain in 1996 by
Parragon Book Service Ltd
Unit 13–17
Avonbridge Trading Estate
Atlantic Road
Avonmouth
Bristol BS11 9QD

First published 1996
Paperback edition published 1997

ISBN: 0-7525-0093-7 (hbk)
ISBN: 0-7525-2148-9 (pbk)


Edited, designed and produced by Haldane Mason

***Editorial Director:*** Sydney Francis
***Art Director:*** Ron Samuels
***Editor:*** Diana Vowles
***Special Photography:*** Amanda Heywood
***Model:*** Cara Hobday


Colour reproduction by Regent Publishing Services, Hong Kong

Printed in Italy by Garzanti-Verga

<u>IMPORTANT</u>

The information, recipes and remedies contained in this book are generally
applicable and appropriate in most cases, but are not tailored to specific
circumstances or individuals. The authors and publishers cannot be held
responsible for any problems arising from the mistaken identity of any plants
or remedies, or the inappropriate use of any remedy or recipe. Do not
undertake any form of self diagnosis or treatment for serious complaints
without first seeking professional advice. Always seek professional medical
advice if symptoms persist.

# Contents

# Introduction

IN TODAY'S WORLD OF CHEMICAL POLLUTION, poisoned rivers and concern about the thinning ozone layer, a way of life that draws on simple, natural elements is increasingly attractive. We have discovered that so-called wonder drugs are often a mixed blessing, bringing a range of sometimes unsuspected side-effects in their wake, and a bottle of little pills doled out by the chemist no longer seems to be necessarily the best option. Obviously there are many illnesses for which the full panoply of conventional medicine is the only answer, but it is possible to effect a home cure for a number of everyday ailments by employing the simple, practical remedies described in this book. Some of them have been used for thousands of years and are still in use because they have proved their worth over and over again in solving health problems. No matter what ailment we may suffer from, we can always do something ourselves to enhance our well-being.

*Ginger*

Ideally, this would be a book of self-sufficient 'bush' remedies, employing local herbage – natural remedies from the local, natural environment. However, many of us live in cities, and even those who live in the country are discouraged from picking plant material by the fear that it has been sprayed by agri-chemicals and lead from car exhausts. Gathering from the wild also requires extensive knowledge and care, so this book draws on what can be found in the home and kitchen, the local shop or supermarket. This covers a large range, for shops everywhere sell herbs and spices that were once rare and expensive, and most kitchens contain a fabulous collection of natural resources that would have been the envy of an 18th-century apothecary. We have the wealth of the world at our fingertips, a priceless natural heritage to enrich our lives and maintain our good health.

## A SHORT HISTORY OF DOMESTIC REMEDIES

When patients telephone to ask me to visit, no matter how urgent the request may be I ask what they have on hand in the kitchen so that I can say 'sage gargle' or 'potato poultice' to start the process of healing while I am on my way. Long-term patients expect this question and gradually accumulate a stock of useful ingredients. Even late on a Sunday or on a public holiday a simple and safe remedy can be made. The kitchen becomes an extension of the bathroom medicine chest, a resource from which to draw help for ourselves and for others.

When Sir Edmund Hillary was asked why he climbed Everest he said, 'Because it was there.' This is also why we smell a rose, watch a bird or gaze at a clear blue sky. These things 'being there' grant us the sensations of being alive. We and the world are complex and inter-active, interdependently relating on many levels, some obvious, some almost imperceptible. Our surroundings either enhance our quality of life and feelings of wellbeing or depress us and our immune system. In this sense everything that delights the senses is medicine: the flowers in spring, the ripple of a river, sunshine on a cornfield.

The ability to make a remedy from local surroundings is one of the most basic skills of life. It is the result of a dialogue with the natural world, and most human societies exercise it in the form of folk or 'bush' remedies and self-sufficient health care. In the developed world, however, much of this knowledge was lost during the industrial revolution, when people uprooted themselves from their traditional rural homes and moved into a city – an alien environment sometimes described as 'a jungle'. Today, there are many barriers between us and a simple appreciation of the world.

Over the centuries, simply 'being there' was rejected as a valid reason for existence, and plants and animals were required to justify their existence by being 'good for' something. Useful features were identified and developed through selective cultivation; cabbages and carnations, for example, were both wild plants until they were improved. This was a rejection of bio-diversity in favour of biological-specialization, a narrowing of being and purpose. It is an insult when we say of a person that they are only good for one thing, yet we doom millions of plants to this fate and rob ourselves of many of their qualities.

All natural things fill an ecological niche or they would not be here. Although I have had to use the 'good for' terminology in some places, the aim of this book is to introduce herbs, spices and vegetables in their own right so that we can use them with knowledge and respect. This book can only begin to describe a small part of the way in which these natural products affect us.

*Published in 1526, this was one of the earliest printed herbals. It was written in English rather than Latin so that anyone, not just monks and priests, could attain 'knowledge and understanding of all manner of herbs and their gracious virtues' in a practical manner.*

*Cinnamon*

The current need to broaden our perceptions is in response to the reductionist philosophies of the past 300 years. It is realized now that we live in an ecological continuum and must be aware of our interdependencies. Ideas and definitions are widening, an interesting example of this being the change in attitude towards aspirin. The recommended dose of aspirin for a headache is 2–4 tablets. Many considered aspirin to be inactive in a lower dosage, but it is now known that taking ½ a tablet daily thins the blood and helps prevent strokes and heart attacks, 1 tablet daily acts as an anti-inflammatory, and at 2 tablets the analgesic property becomes evident. These actions are the progressive physiological interactions of aspirin within the human body, and if too much is taken it causes stomach bleeds. Yet just ten years ago aspirin was defined solely as 'good for' headaches.

For hygiene and convenience everything now comes in packages, but each piece of cardboard or clingfilm (plastic wrap) creates an extra distance between us and the natural state of the product. Soft drink comes in cans or bottles independent of rain cycles, and packets of strawberries appear on the shelves irrespective of weather or season. Some city children do not even realize that milk comes from cows, or that chips are from the potato plant. Such ignorance is dangerous, for we are totally dependent on plants for our existence, for the oxygen we breathe. Conservation is not just about dolphins, whales and the tropical rainforest; it is to do with the health of the plants we use daily. To nourish and maintain us, plants must be healthy themselves. Dead plants, over-sprayed herbs, irradiated spices and chemical substitutes do not enrich us.

Look at the kitchen shelves and the natural riches on display, the diversity of leaves, stems, bark, roots, tubers, seeds, fruits,

nuts and fibres. Taking ingredients out of their packets and back into the real world begins with this awareness of what things are in themselves and recognition of their unique qualities. For example, lemons are sharp, cooling and acid. The skin contains an insect-repellent and a strong, oily antiseptic. There are many ways in which we can make use of these qualities: the mild acids can clean metal, bleach linen, whiten skin and lighten hair; the peel can disinfect, repel insects, discourage moths, or be used as an antiseptic; the pips can kill parasitic worms and also produce another lemon tree. This is just a general appreciation, without taking into consideration the lemon's constituents like vitamin C and its remedial virtues.

Although the earth is abundant we have a responsibility to use the resources wisely and without unnecessary waste. Native Americans demonstrated the comprehension of their world typical of traditional cultures by honouring their 'natural relatives'. They showed a complete understanding of the property and being of buffalo by using everything – the hide, flesh, skin, teeth and hooves. The same can be true of plants, although in Europe a more pragmatic understanding is at the root of, for example, the use of nettle. This plant is employed for making dyes, fibre, linen, rope and paper, and for medicine and tonic. Boswell describes Dr Johnson eating nettle pudding from a table laid with nettle cloth, dyed nettle green. Let us toast them in nettle beer!

In primitive times humans had to learn how to interact with flora and fauna. It was important to identify the entire character of a plant, as some would prove to be poisonous or have unexpected hallucinatory properties. Knowledge was acquired by trial and error. It is amazing to consider a plant such as cassava; if eaten raw it is poisonous to humans and animals, yet after careful preparation and repeated or prolonged boiling it becomes edible. For many people it is a staple – but how was it learned that cooking it rendered it safe? However it was obtained, such wisdom and experience was passed to the next generation by means of oral tradition and, later, manuscripts.

As the world became more complicated, specialization became the thing. 'As theories increased, simple medicines were more and more disregarded and disused, till in a course of years the greater part of them were forgotten, at least in politer nations. In the room of these abundances new ones were introduced by reasoning speculative and remote

*Parsley*

from common observation . . . medical books immensely multiplied till at length physic became abstruse science quite out of the reach of the ordinary man.' This was written in 1840 by Dr Coffin, an American who was cured of a life-threatening disease by Native American medicine and subsequently became a champion of botanic medicine in Britain. Scientific understanding has now become so detailed that it is possible for an expert to understand the molecular chemistry of something like a lemon without ever needing to know its shape, colour or taste.

While the scientific community pursued knowledge and the guilds developed into professions, the majority of people still had to continue to care for themselves and their families. Some experts wrote books for the layman – the most famous example being Culpeper's *Herbal*, which has been continually reprinted since 1652 – but people also compiled books for themselves, listing the skill and plant knowledge they needed to survive.

A woman in charge of a large house or large family had to have a huge range of practical and administrative skills. She needed a sound and intimate knowledge of her natural surroundings to be able to make do, to find, to stretch and substitute, to respond flexibly whatever the situation or season. In the houses of the gentlefolk this precious experience was written into household, or still-room, books to be passed on, together with tips, timesavers, recipes and comments. 'Mary Doggett; her book of receipts' (1682) is a good example. There is no room here to give any recipes, but just a few of the titles convey the extent of her duties and extensive housekeeping skills: 'Grapes in jelly'; 'To preserve blew violets for Salletts'; 'Almond milk'; 'Plasters for bruises'; 'Balme water'; 'To perfume gloves in the Spanish manner'; 'Sweet powders for linen'; 'Orange biskett'; 'Orange butter'; 'To keep Cherrys all year'; 'Paste for the hands'; 'Pickle cucumbers'; 'To candy oranges or lemons or any kind of sucketts'; 'To make cowslip wine'; 'Drinks to cause sleep'; 'A perfume for a sweet bag'.

Some of these recipes are similar to the recipes in this book, and many of the methods are the same; the traditions and skills are still valuable and relevant. These still-room books run parallel to the learned texts of the scientists, and contain the everyday knowledge needed not only to survive in harmony with nature but to get the best from life. The golden age of these books is from the late 17th century, when every great house would have had one.

The earliest still-room book is called 'A choice manual of rare and selected Secrets in Physick and Chirurgerie Collected and practised by the Countess of Kent' (1651). Her notes based on personal experience are not only interesting but vital to the success of the remedy. One of the formulas ends, 'Take three time as the first helpeth not.' It is this sort of empirical learning, wrought from trial and error, which it is so important to pass on. In this way we are able to learn from each other.

*Fennel seed*

The authors of the still-room books swapped recipes and ideas. Some remedies were traded freely, others were secret and became the subject of gossip and intrigue. In 'The Lady Sedley her Receipt Book', one recipe is introduced thus: 'A copy to make the [most] sovereign water that ever was devised by man, which Dr. Stephens a physician of great cunning and of long experience did use and therewith did cure many great cases, and all was kept in secret until a little before his death; when the archbishop of Canterbury got it from him'. It is not recorded how the Archbishop accomplished this task!

Lady Sedley's book has recipes that were gained from most of the famous personages of the time, including the three doctors who attended Charles II. Another recipe is from the ill-fated Duke of Monmouth. History is humanized when we picture these great men and women who were involved in the complexities and intrigues of state swapping recipes and worrying about their spots and mildew. History usually only recounts the major events of the dominant culture, but in still-room books the past becomes real as we witness the trials and tribulations of life, the domestic concerns and small victories over the everyday problems that we all share.

*Garlic*

The most famous still-room book written by a man is that by Sir Kenelm Digby, the eldest son of one of the Gunpowder Plot conspirators. He was a friend of kings, a philosopher, man of science, doctor, occultist, privateer and herbalist. He numbered all the eminent people of Europe as his friends and collected assiduously from them, with credit and pride. His collection includes 'Scotch ale from my Lady Holmeby'; 'Master Webb's Ale and Bragot'; 'Sir Paul Neal's way of making cider'; 'Meathe from the Muscovian Ambassador's steward'; 'My Lord of St Alban's Cresme Fouettee'; and even 'The Queen's Barley cream'.

*Honey*

The example of 'My Lady Barclay's Apple-jelly', shows the precise detail in which such things were discussed.

'My Lady Barclay makes her fine Apple-jelly with slices of John Apples. Sometimes she mingles a few pippins with the Johns to make the jelly. But she likes best the Johns single and the colour is paler. You first fill the glass with slices round-wise cut, and then the jelly is poured in to fill up the vacuities. The jelly must be boiled to a good stiffness. Then when it is ready to take from the fire, you put in some juice of Lemon, and of Orange too, if you like it, but these must not boil; yet it must stand a while upon the fire stewing in good heat, to have the juices incorporated and penetrate well. You must also put in some Ambergris, which doth exceedingly well in this sweet meat.'

As civilizations rise and fall, many skills are learned and then forgotten. Many things that are mentioned in an offhand manner in books because they were thought common knowledge are today totally unknown, for example major inventions such as Greek fire or small household things such as the famous ancient Roman Paste, once eaten with almost everything. Some plants which are described in the 18th century as 'so common I shall not bother to describe' are now believed to be extinct. Indeed, many of the skills known as recently as our grandparents' generation are already forgotten. This is sad, as we should be building on their foundations, not having to start anew every generation. There is much to learn about our natural environment, lessons from our own observations and 'accidents'.

Dr Coffin believed in happy 'accidents'. He recounts: '[A man] walking some years since, in a grove of pines, at the time when many of the neighbouring towns were afflicted with a kind of new distemper [little sores in the inside of the mouth], a drop of the natural gum fell from one of the trees on the book which he was reading; this he took up, and thoughtlessly applied to one of the sore places. Finding the pain immediately cease, he applied it to another, which also presently healed. The same remedy he afterwards imparted to others and it did not fail to heal any that applied it.' He adds 'and doubtless numberless remedies have been thus casually discovered in every age and nation'.

It is important to us as a species that we share. We are all interested to see how we each survive, develop life-styles and stratagems, express wellbeing and a joy of life through the arts, so start a household book for your family. Write down your experiences in detail, for who knows what may be important in years to come? Include favourite recipes, remedies from this book, tips, information and comments. Treasure your personal and family skills, health regimes and traditions. Take from the past, enjoy the present and add your voice to the future.

*Marigold*

# How to Use this Book

This book does not lay down firm rules or give specific instructions, for the treatment suitable for one person may not be good for another. It has only half the information needed for accurate self care; you have the other half.

All substances, even the most benign, affect someone, somewhere, adversely. For example, chamomile is one of the mildest herbs and is ideally suited to children, but very occasionally a child has an idiopathic reaction, a mild nausea. There is no way of determining the person or the reaction; chamomile must simply be taken with the awareness that certain rare individuals will demonstrate an intolerance. This book has the general information that chamomile is a mild, gentle herb, but you have the specific knowledge needed to use it. You are the expert on your body and its tolerances and intolerances. If you feel uneasy about a remedy, or know from experience that it does not suit you, do not take it, even if the greatest brains in the universe recommend it.

No plant can be guaranteed to be entirely harmless, as plants are complex with complex actions. For example, garlic is a hot, odorous antiseptic. This will be its action within the body. This action can be balanced with other herbs; the odour can be moderated with parsley, the heat accentuated with cayenne or cooled with cabbage. The body will respond to the entire 'character' of garlic. This has to be accepted when taking a remedy.

Everything in this book is tried and tested, but the final responsibility is yours. Listen to your body and learn by experience – general and specific knowledge working together will produce useful health-care stratagems.

Listening to our bodies is hard. We are all poor at taking care of ourselves. In our practice we hear such excuses as, 'I've been sick all night. I knew there was something fishy about the fish, but I did not want to embarrass my host.' 'It's my own fault. I got chilled to the bone. I was too tired and cold when I got home to make myself ginger tea.' 'I always get PMT on the months when my diet is poor and I am too busy to eat. I know I should eat some carbohydrate every four hours.'

Why does this happen? Women especially practise a type of empathy that monitors the health, mood and emotional well-being of friends and loved ones. This sophisticated tool is seldom turned on themselves. We must apply the skills and compassion that we extend to our loved ones to ourselves.

Once you have accepted a greater responsibility for your own health, act to effect a change. Make a few teas and begin to learn about the character of the herbs and spices in a general way. Use them more in cooking. Try some everyday recipes, make hand baths, oat washes and tonics. Add the information in this book to your understanding of yourself and your body. Later, take walks and notice the plants growing and how they contribute toward

enriching life. Let these 'herbal remedies' please the eye and raise the spirits.

The art of living in harmony with our planet is an evolving discipline, not a dead science. We must be grateful to all those who over the ages took the time to pass on their experience, whether through oral traditions or still-room books and herbals. Worldwide, there exists a huge canon of plant lore, though it is often not generally acknowledged. In 1994 the botanist Gabrielle Hatfield published a survey into the current use of country remedies in East Anglia, England. She reported: 'After the great advances of modern medicine over the past fifty years, it comes as a surprise to discover that so many remedies are still in circulation, even though largely within the over-sixties age group.' The remedies she recorded are simple and universal. Among those she collected for toothache are putting the kernel of an onion in the cavity, using cabbage leaves as a poultice and chewing a clove – all simple and effective remedies that are also mentioned in this book. She concluded that this is a critical time for folk medicine if we do not want to lose our experience of plants which have proved their efficacy over centuries.

Understanding the plants and remedies around us provides a sense of unity, place, purpose and belonging. Use this book to care for yourself, your loved ones, the plants, and the planet which ultimately provides sustenance for us all.

# MAKING
# ❧ REMEDIES ❧

*Whatever the condition or situation, it's always
possible to do something, whether simply holding
a hand or giving more practical help. There is
nothing quite like the satisfaction of tending loved
ones with natural home-made remedies. This
chapter gives easy step-by-step instructions for
making a wide range of home remedies, from a
simple tisane to massage oils and herb salts.*

# Making Remedies

It may seem a lot of trouble to buy fresh ingredients or herbs and brew them up yourself when a proprietary remedy can be bought at the chemists and downed in an instant. However, there is no substitute for freshness and quality, and it is healing in itself to live in balance with nature rather than simply taking a pill. There is also the fact that home remedies are usually cheaper!

Most kitchens already contain the basics for a simple self-care pharmacy and making a remedy is no more complicated than making tea and toast or boiling an egg. It is also an expression of shared concern for a member of the family who is ailing, which is a comfort in a way that unwrapping a packet of proprietary medicine could never be.

Unless a herb is eaten fresh or bruised and applied directly as a poultice, some method of extraction of its goodness is needed. In many European countries, country people eat sage leaves with bread and butter and say that there is no better way of taking it. This may be true for a general tonic, but for a sore throat, for example, a sage gargle would be better.

There are many different methods of preparation and many factors to consider when deciding which one to use. The method may be dictated by the ailment itself, or by the simplicity of use and the availability of fresh ingredients. Remedies may need to be preserved for regular use. Convenience may also be an issue: if chamomile is to be taken four times a day, a tincture or decoction may be easier to carry and take than a cup of tea. Finally, a particular method may enhance the action of the herbs themselves, as in the case of onion syrup, where the soothing, antiseptic honey brings out the demulcent, expectorant properties of the onion.

The country people may be happy with their sage sandwiches, but in *The English Physician* (1694), the first common herbal for home use, the famous herbalist Culpeper

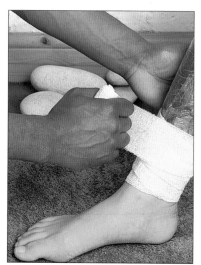

*Vinegar and brown paper – a traditional remedy so effective it is enshrined in the children's nursery rhyme 'Jack and Jill'.*

*Tinctures preserve the properties of the fresh herb or spice in alcohol, for use all through the year.*

suggests several methods to bring out the full therapeutic action of sage:

✻ **'Juice with honey, taken fasting:** stays spitting blood . . . in consumption.'

✻ **'Pills made with sage juice and sage ashes:** all kinds of pains in the head coming of cold and rheumatic humours; . . . lowness of spirits, and the palsy.'

✻ **'Decoction:** provokes urine, expels the dead child and brings down women's courses. It stays the bleeding of wounds and cleanses foul ulcers . . . Causes the hair to become black.'

✻ **'Bruised leaves as a poultice:** imposthumes that rise behind the ears, assuages them much.'

✻ **'Juice in warm water:** helps hoarseness and a cough.'

✻ **'Leaves sodden in wine as a poultice:** the palsy.'

✻ **'Juice drank with vinegar:** for the plague.'

✻ **'Boiled in wine:** gargles, sore mouths and throats.'

✻ **'Boiled in water with other comforting herbs:** bathe body to warm cold joints troubled with palsy and cramp, and to strengthen the parts.'

✻ **'Fomentation:** Stitch or pains in the side coming from wind.'

✻ **'Conserve of the flowers:** aiding memory, warming and quickening the senses.'

In this section of the book there are detailed instructions for making a whole range of herbal preparations. The methods can be divided into:

1 Water-based extractions, infusions and decoctions, which are used as teas, gargles, washes, lotions, douches and syrups;

2 Spirit-based extractions and tinctures using wine, spirits or vinegar;

3 Oil extractions, which make bath and body oils, ointments, creams, plaisters, liniments, salves and pessaries.

Making remedies involves organic chemistry. The practice is simple, the theory complex. Cooking is practical organic chemistry in action, but it is not necessary to explain the principles of our physical universe to make coffee and waffles, although we demonstrate them daily. Understanding cookery comes from a familiarity with the ingredients and empirical expertise, and

*It is easy to make skin and hair care preparations at home using everyday ingredients and materials.*

the same is true of making home remedies. Follow the recipes to start with and gradually learn to know the herb or spice, its smell, taste, feel, texture, actions, qualities and virtues. Is it hot or cold? What does it go with? Know it intellectually and intuitively so that the herb becomes a trusted friend and you have confidence in it.

When you are responding to a family ailment, decide on the herbs or spices to use and then the method of preparation. Remember the reasons for making the remedy and the added value that comes from home-made preparations: individual treatment, love and care. Once you have started to make remedies, buy a notebook and start a Family Health Book – a modern version of a still-room book. Write in recipes and cost, tips on making and comments on any interesting detail. This will become invaluable to you and will be a useful and interesting document to pass on to children and grandchildren. Throughout these recipes, names appear in the titles, records of a particular cure that proved efficacious for a particular person. Let your Family Health Book act as a similar record of your successes in curing those whom you care for.

*There is a medicinal use for every herb and spice found in the kitchen, whether in a tincture or decoction, or simply in a fragrant pot pourri for use around the home.*

# Water Infusions

**W**HEN PLANT MATERIAL IS INFUSED IN WATER, *the water becomes a fragrantly scented and pleasantly refreshing drink known as 'tea'. However, tea is more than just an enjoyable means of quenching thirst. Our bodies are 90 per cent water and we have an intimate affinity with this element. Teas are potent medicine as well as being easy to assimilate and digest, and when diluted they are suitable for children and even the most delicate of stomachs.*

*'Tea' is usually taken to mean the dried and cured leaves of the plant Camellia sinensis, a member of the family Theaceae. It is grown in China, India, Sri Lanka, South-East Asia, Africa and South America, different soils and climates producing different flavours. This is regarded as the classic tea, but in fact any plant may be used, on its own or in a blend. Before 'tea' became dominant, herb, spice and fruit teas were common.*

*To drink the tea, hold it so that the steam and fragrance can be inhaled. Take a sip and notice the flavours. Once it is drunk, note the effects spreading out from the stomach.*

## Option

*Water infusions at standard tea strength can be used as gargles, lotions, douches, compresses, rinses and fomentations. To make a fomentation, dilute the tea with 1 litre/1¾ pints/4 cups of hot water, dip a cloth in, squeeze out excess liquid and apply. Fomentations improve circulation, draw abscesses and warm cold and stiff joints.*

**INGREDIENTS**

1 teaspoon herbs

❧

250 ml/8 fl oz/1 cup boiling water

**DOSE**

Tonic: 1–2 times a day

Standard treatment: 3 times a day

Acute conditions: 6 times a day

1 Chop the herbs, either fresh or dried. Tea-making is an art, and there are many elements involved in creating a good blend: taste, nose, astringency and fore- and aftertaste. Bear this in mind when trying to make a pleasant medicinal blend. Some herbs work together, some clash, so experiment. Calming Heaven digestive tea is a good example of balanced flavours. Take 15 g/½ oz parsley, 8 g/¼ oz fennel, 8 g/¼ oz peppermint and ½ teaspoon ground ginger.

2 Draw fresh water, as the pouring aerates it. Only draw the amount you need. If you live in an area with good tap water this will suffice, otherwise a still mineral water can be used. There are many different mineral waters and it is a matter of personal taste which one you use. Distilled water, although pure, has a flat, lifeless taste. As soon as the water comes to the boil, pour it over the herbs and cover with a tight lid.

3 Leave the tea to brew so that elements in the herbs seep into the water. Allow 1–3 minutes for flowers, 2–4 minutes for leaves and 4–10 minutes for seeds, bark and hard roots. Cover the pot with a cosy to retain the heat if brewing for longer than 4 minutes. Strain the tea into a teacup. (Tea is supposed to taste better if served in fine bone china.)

4 Milk is rarely used in herbal teas as it tends to suppress the flavour. If you do use it, remember to pour the milk first and then stir in the tea, otherwise the milk may scald and spoil the tea. Honey, lemon juice or a pinch of cayenne pepper may all be added to bring out the particular properties of a tea. For example, honey in sage tea soothes the throat, or cayenne in sage helps break a fever.

5 Herbal teas can be drunk warm, hot, cold or iced. The temperature brings out special effects, depending on the herb. For example, hot sage tea before bed promotes sweating, helping to break a fever; iced sage tea cools the system, acting as a refreshing tonic and diminishing sweating. In general, hot teas tend to warm and stimulate the circulation; at room temperature they are neutral; iced they are cooling.

# Decoctions

A DECOCTION IS AN EXTRACT OF HERBS *produced by boiling the herb in water. This method is used for hard seeds, roots and barks, which need longer than an infusion. It is also a method of reducing and preserving water extracts. There is something very harmonious and healing about using this medium. It is the best for children and persons with a weakened constitution. Although decoctions are prepared by prolonged simmering, they still contain the essential qualities of the fresh herb.*
*Decoctions are extremely versatile. They can be drunk on their own, made into syrups, honeys, gargles, compresses and douches, added to baths or used as an ingredient in oils and creams.*

**INGREDIENTS**

**40 g/1½ oz dried or
60 g/2½ oz fresh herb**

❋

**900 ml/1½ pints/3¾ cups
boiling water**

**DOSE**

**50 ml/2 fl oz/¼ cup 2–3 times a day**

1 Crush and bruise the herbs in a pestle and mortar. Put the herbs in a bowl and cover with the boiling water. Leave to stand overnight. (There are a number of slightly different ways of making a decoction: the water may be hot or cold and standing overnight is a variable. Try this method first; later you can experiment and compare.)

2 In the morning, put the herb and water into a saucepan. Make the liquid back up to 900 ml/1½ pints/3¾ cups (some will have soaked into the herb). Bring it to the boil. Once it is bubbling, turn the heat right down so that the mixture just simmers. Put the lid on the pan and simmer gently for 20 minutes.

**3** Remove from the heat and strain through a jelly bag or a fine cloth in a strainer. Squeeze out all the liquid and discard the herbs. This is a standard decoction, which will keep for 2–3 days and can be taken neat.

**4** To make a reduced decoction, pour the liquid into a measuring pan or pouring pan and return to the heat. Heat gently until it begins to steam. Once you see the steam rising, turn the heat down very low and let the liquid steam until it is reduced to 200 ml/7 fl oz/⁷⁄₈ cup. If the pan has internal measuring marks use them, or you can estimate by watching the rings the liquid makes as it evaporates (or use a ruler). Slow evaporation takes about 1½ hours per 600 ml/ 1 pint/2½ cups. When the liquid is sufficiently reduced, allow to cool, pour into clean bottles, label and date. A reduced decoction will keep for 4–5 days in a cool place.

*Simple decoctions, like this bottle of rosemary, can be used on their own, as they contain the essential qualities of the fresh herbs. Pour a cup of boiling water over 1–2 tablespoons of rosemary decoction to produce a drink as vital as fresh tea. The fragrance of the herb, digestive warmth, circulatory stimulant properties, general head-clearing and tonic properties are all easily perceived.*

# Preserving decoctions

*Decoctions can be preserved indefinitely by:*

1 *Adding 450 g/1 lb honey or sugar to 200 ml/7 fl oz/ ⅞ cup of decoction. Dose: 1 teaspoon 3 times a day.*
2 *Adding spirits at a proportion of 2 parts decoction to 1 part spirit. Dose: 50 ml/ 2 fl oz/ ¼ cup 2 times a day.*
3 *Floating a thin film of vegetable oil over the surface and sealing. This will keep for about a year. To use, either draw off the oil or pour the decoction from beneath it. Dose: ½–1 tsp 3 times a day.*

4 *Making a thick fluid extract by reducing to 25ml/ 1 fl oz/1¾ tablespoons. In a temperate climate a simple reduced fluid extract will keep for months, if not years. Dose: 1–3 drops 3 times a day.*

*A fluid extract is reconstituted thus:*
*Decoction strength: 1 part fluid extract : 10 parts water*
*Infusion strength: 1 part fluid extract : 25 parts water.*
*Once reconstituted it is treated in the same manner as normal decoctions and infusions, with the same dosages.*

# Tinctures

In a **TINCTURE THE PROPERTIES OF THE HERB** *are extracted and preserved in alcohol. In early times this was achieved by boiling the herb in wine. There are many old recipes of a handful of this and a handful of that, boiled in a barrelful of wine and drunk freely.*

*Tinctures can be made with fresh or dried ingredients. Although some herbs need different strengths of alcohol (15–90 per cent proof), the following ratio is a suitable standard for home use: 25 g/1 oz dried herb or 50 g/2 oz fresh to 600 ml/ 1 pint/2½ cups alcoholic liquid. Tinctures keep indefinitely and the dosage is small and effective. For those unable to take alcohol, put the dose in 50 ml/2 fl oz/¼ cup water and leave uncovered for several hours while the alcohol evaporates.*

*When plenty of fresh herbs become available each year, this is the time to start collecting clean jars and bottles to take advantage of the supply. Add herbs and spices to a bottle of wine – a light white or rosé is best, as this allows the fragrance of the herbs to flavour the wine gently. Drink when needed. Spiced wines may be diluted with water or fruit juices and served cold, iced or mulled. A pleasant spiced wine includes a sprig of fresh rosemary, 4 cardamom seeds, 4 cloves and a twist of lemon peel.*

21

**INGREDIENTS**
Makes 200–300 ml/7–10 fl oz/
⁷⁄₈–1¹⁄₄ cups
✤
15g/¹⁄₂oz dried herbs
✤
200 ml/7 fl oz/⁷⁄₈ cup spirit
such as vodka or brandy
✤
85 ml/3 fl oz/6 tablespoons water

**DOSE**

**Tonic: 5 drops–1 teaspoon once a day**

**Standard treatment: 1 teaspoon 3 times a day**

**Acute conditions: 1 teaspoon 6 times a day**

**Diluted: 1 teaspoon of tincture to 250 ml/8 fl oz/1 cup water to make a gargle, wash or compress**

1 Chop or bruise the herb (in this case sage). Mix together the spirit and the water.

2 Put the herb into a large jar and add the alcoholic liquid. Label and date the jar and leave to stand in a cool, dark place for 2 weeks. Shake or turn upside-down daily.

3 After 2 weeks the liquid will have drawn out the goodness of the herb and changed colour. It is tempting to leave the mixture to stand for longer. Do not do so – it does not strengthen the tincture, and the herb begins to break down chemically. Strain through a loose-weave cotton cloth placed in a sieve (strainer).

4 Squeeze and wring the herbs in the cloth to get out every drop of precious liquid – this is the tincture. Discard the spent herbs.

5 Pour the strained liquid into clean glass bottles – amber glass is best. Make sure the bottles, and their lids, are really clean. They can be boiled, sterilized in a pressure cooker or soaked in a sterilizing liquid for babies' bottles. In clean bottles a tincture will keep indefinitely. Label the bottles clearly with the name of the tincture, the date made, the dosage and some indication of use.

# Tonic wines and spirits

*This is a pleasant way of taking tonic herbs over a long period of time. When fresh herbs are in season make enough for the year. Use 25 g/1 oz herbs and 50 g/ 2 oz spices to 2 litres/3½ pints/ 7½ cups red or white wine or alcoholic liquid made with 2 parts spirits to 1 part water. Make in the same way as a tincture. Take 50 ml/2 fl oz/ ¼ cup twice a day. Warm water may be added to taste. Tonic wines also stimulate the appetite when taken as an aperitif 20 minutes before eating.*

# Vinegars

VINEGAR IS A SECONDARY BACTERIAL FERMENTATION OF ALCOHOL, *made previously by a yeast fermentation. It is weaker than spirits but is much cheaper, better tolerated and more in keeping with the acid pH of the skin. It is useful for skin and hair preparations, washes and douches.*
*There are many types of vinegar, including wine, sherry, cider and malt. Acetic acid is often substituted but this is a pity, as natural vinegar is full of rich fragrances and subtle undertones. There are connoisseurs of vinegars as dedicated as those who savour wine or real ale. In herbal medicine wine and cider vinegars are favoured for their gentle action.*
*To obtain all the trace elements, vitamins and flavour, make vinegar from a vinegar 'mother'. Traditionally, these were passed from generation to generation. Many European villages made vinegars as distinctive as their local wines.*
*Once started, a vinegar culture must be maintained and fed. The ideal container is a widemouthed earthenware crock. Use scrupulously clean utensils to prevent contamination.*

## Cider vinegar

> **INGREDIENTS**
>
> waste apple peel and cores
> ❧
> enough water to cover

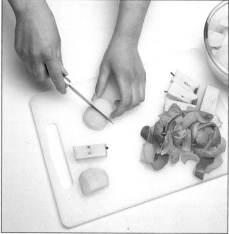

1 Scrub the apples thoroughly in plenty of water. There is plenty of goodness just below the peel, but make sure that the peel itself is clean and free from preservative waxes and pesticide residues. Use organic apples whenever possible.

2 Peel and core the apples. All types of apples are suitable, but use just one variety as each imparts a slightly different flavour to the vinegar: Russets and Granny Smiths nutty, Cox's sweet and woody and Bramleys clear and invigorating.

**3** Use the flesh of the apples as desired. Put the apple peel and cores in a wide-mouthed crock or jar and just cover with pure water. Cover the crock, put in a warm place and leave to ferment. This recipe works best with the core and peels of at least 12 apples. If using much less than this, add ¼ cup apple juice – this means less water will be needed to cover.

**4** Taste the liquid every few days and stir to aerate. Remove the froth as it ferments. The taste of vinegar will develop gradually (depending on temperature) and the cloudiness of the liquid will clear. When it is to your taste it is ready to strain into a large bowl. Empty the crock in preparation for the next batch – it may need to be rinsed with water or wiped, but never use detergent or soap. To make a fresh batch, add fresh apple peel and cores, add the vinegar mother and enough water to cover. Repeat steps 1–4.

*Pour the mojority of the vinegar into a bottle and label it with the date. Once the vinegar has reached a full vinegar taste there is no more alcohol to ferment and it becomes a stabilized product. When bottled, the vinegar should not deteriorate. Return a small amount of vinegar to the crock to become the vinegar 'mother' of future vinegars. To keep the vinegar mother 'alive' until you next wish to make vinegar, add peel and water occasionally to the liquid left in the crock.*

# Quick wine vinegar

## Red cabbage with vinegar

*This recipe is simple to make and can be used hot or cold. All you need is red cabbage, cider vinegar, the juice of an orange and 1 teaspoon of caraway seeds. Boil all the ingredients together until the cabbage is soft. This could also be applied as a compress to good effect.*

**1** Put the wine or sherry in a crock and add the barley. Stand in a warm place for a few days.

**Right:** *When it tastes right (usually after 2–3 days) strain and bottle. Label the bottle. Keep some of the liquid and return it to the crock. This becomes a 'starter' or 'mother'. To maintain her in good health, feed occasionally with dregs of wine. Always use the same type of wine, red or white.*

# Vinegar hair rinse

*A vinegar hair rinse keeps the scalp healthy and the hair conditioned. Dilute 1 tablespoon of herbal vinegar with 250 ml/ 8 fl oz/1 cup of water. Rub thoroughly into the hair and scalp. Leave for 5 minutes, then rinse off.*

*Use sage to darken hair, chamomile or lemon to lighten it, parsley to cure dandruff and rosemary to condition dry, thin or falling hair.*

---

# Medicinal vinegar tinctures

*Use your vinegar to make medicinal vinegar tinctures. These are made in the same way and the same proportions as tinctures (see page 21). They are also taken in the same doses.*

# Spiced vinegar

*Spice vinegars are easy to make and use. In cooking they bring out the delicate flavour of herbs and add an individual taste to salad dressings. They make refreshing drinks, skin lotions and hair rinses. To use as a douche, dilute 2 teaspoons of vinegar in 250 ml/8 fl oz/1 cup tepid water.*

# Fruit vinegar

Cover the fruit with vinegar, leave to stand for 2 weeks then strain and bottle the liquid. Fruit vinegars are best made when soft fruits and berries are plentiful, so that their minerals and vitamins are preserved for use during the cold, dark winter. Dose: 1 teaspoon to a cup of water, or to taste. Fruit vinegar is sharpening and cleansing first thing in the morning – a 'wake up' tonic for the whole system. In winter they are used to ease coughs and colds, to cut phlegm and to soothe fevers. Iced fruit vinegar is cooling and refreshing on a hot summer day.

# Sage and vinegar poultice

*Vinegar brings bruises to the surface, cooling and reducing swelling. Sage and vinegar are both traditional ingredients in compresses. Used together, they are unsurpassed for easing sprains.*

*'Sage is singularly good for the head and braine; it quickens the senses and memory, strengtheneth the sinews, restoreth health to those that have the palsie, takes away shaking or trembling of the members.'*

**John Gerard,** *The Herball or Generall Historie of Plants,* **1597**

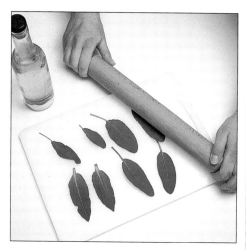

**1** Bruise whole, fresh sage leaves by flattening them with a rolling pin. Try not to break or tear them.

**2** Put the sage leaves in a pan and just cover with vinegar. Simmer gently for 5 minutes over a very low heat. The vinegar should not boil but it should steam so that the sage leaves soften and blanch.

# Vinegar and brown paper poultice

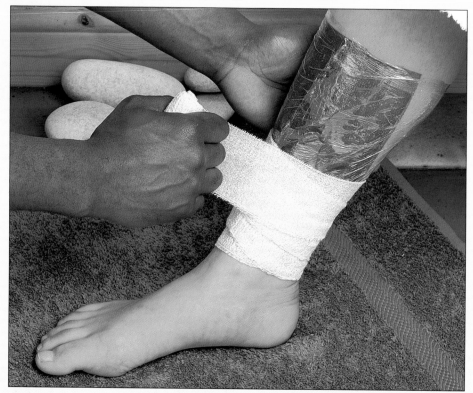

*1 This effective traditional remedy became enshrined in a rhyme because it worked: in the nursery rhyme 'Jack and Jill', Jack 'went to bed to mend his head with vinegar and brown paper'.*

*Put 5 or 6 sheets of strong brown paper in a pan and cover with sage vinegar. Put the lid on the pan and steam over a very low heat for a few minutes. The time will depend on the type of paper. It should soften and absorb some vinegar without breaking or disintegrating.*

*2 Take out the paper and wrap it in overlapping layers around the affected part. Use it as hot as possible and build up several layers. Cover with clingfilm (plastic wrap)* *and bandage. Leave on for 4 hours. Vinegar poultices feel very supportive and strengthening. Reapply twice a day until the swelling and bruising have subsided.*

**3** After 5 minutes, take out the leaves and lay them on a cloth. Work quickly and carefully as the leaves are very hot. Fold the cloth into a package which will just cover the affected area.

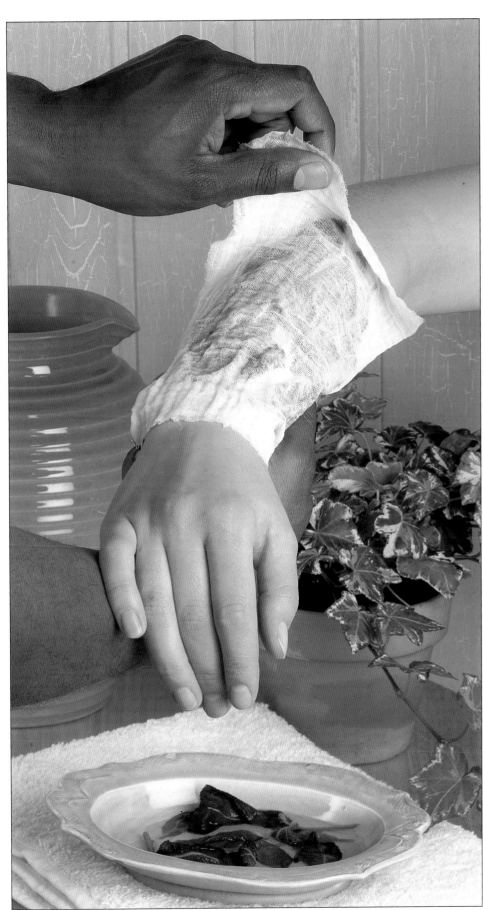

*Apply as hot as can be borne and cover with towels to retain the heat. Leave on for an hour or until the swelling has subsided.*

*Vinegar can also be diluted with warm water and used as a fomentation for sprains and bruises. Diluted with cold or iced water it makes an excellent compress for hot, swollen joints or hot tension headaches.*

# Infused Oils

TO MAKE AN INFUSED OIL, *herbs and spices are heated in a 'fat'*
*base. Traditionally, the base would have been olive oil, clarified*
*butter, hog's fat, goose grease or suet. Today a light, neutral*
*vegetable oil like sunflower oil is most often used, although the*
*healing properties of butter are being reassessed. The recipe*
*and method of infusion is the same for all fats.*
*When heated the oil takes on the therapeutic properties of the*
*herbs and spices. The oil can then be used as a massage oil,*
*rub, bath oil or skin lotion or as a base for an ointment, salve,*
*cream, suppository, plaister or liniment. Dried or fresh*
*ingredients can be used.*

## Rose oil
### Slow sun method

### INGREDIENTS

**fragrant red rose petals (damask
roses are good for this oil)**
✾
**good-quality vegetable oil, such as
cold-pressed olive oil**

*Fill a large jar or bottle with a good vegetable oil. Add red rose petals so that
they are covered with oil but are not tightly packed. Cover with an airtight lid
and leave in direct sunshine. When the petals become brown, remove them and
add fresh blooms. Repeat until the oil is tinged pink. In an uncertain northern
climate this may take 20 or more changes over a summer season. Perseverance
is worthwhile as this method best captures the fragrance of delicate petals.*

# Rosemary oil
## Quick kitchen method

**INGREDIENTS**

Makes approx 300 ml/¹/₂ pint/
1¹/₄ cups infused oil

❀

50–75 g/2–3 oz dried herbs or
75–100 g/3–4 oz fresh

❀

300 ml/¹/₂ pint/1¹/₄ cups
unblended vegetable oil

1 Chop the rosemary. Put half the rosemary and all the oil into a container with a tight lid.

2 Put the container in a pan, fill the pan with water to within 2.5 cm/ 1 inch of the top of the container and simmer slowly for 2 hours. This water bath allows prolonged heating without the danger of spoiling the oil by boiling. To save time and energy costs, 2–3 canisters can be heated together.

3 After 2 hours, allow the mixture to cool slightly and then strain it well. This is now halfway through the process and the oil will have changed colour. At this strength it can be used for infants, either directly on the skin or as a bath oil. Discard the spent herbs – these will make excellent compost once rotted, completing the circle by returning the goodness back to the land.

4 Refill the canister with the remaining rosemary, cover with the strained oil and return to the water bath. Simmer gently for another 2 hours. Don't forget to replace the lid and also to check the water level to make sure that the water has not boiled away. Burnt oil is a frequent occurrence and it has no value at all.

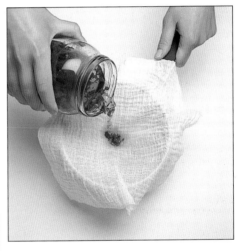

5 When the oil has cooled enough to work with, pour it through a jelly bag or a sieve (strainer) lined with muslin (cheesecloth). If you are using fresh herbs there may be watery green liquid at the bottom of the oil. This liquid must be separated out and thrown away, otherwise it will deteriorate and quickly spoil the oil.

**6** Once the oil has been strained, gather up the herbs in the cloth and wring them out to extract every drop of oil. Although the oil will keep fresh for a year it will eventually become rancid. This can be delayed by adding wheatgerm oil at a proportion of 5–10 per cent.

**7** Pour the oil into clean bottles and label them clearly with the name and date. Store in a cool, dark place. Infused herb oils can be used as they are or as the base for many different preparations.

**Right:** *As oils infuse the healing qualities of the herbs, they also pick up the colours. Infused oils should be stored in dark or amber bottles, but these are photographed in clear glass to show their rich, jewel-like beauty. The oils shown here include marigold, sage and cayenne with paprika.*

# Preparations using infused herb oils

**A solid salve**
*To make a solid salve for chapped, damaged or inflamed skin and for haemorrhoids, thicken the oil into a salve by melting together with beeswax in a ratio of 4:1. Marigold, chamomile and rose oils make excellent salves, as do wild herbs like chickweed (Stellaria media) and plantain (Plantago major).*

**A liniment rub**
*Make a liniment rub for tired and aching limbs by mixing 1 part of herb oil with 1 part herb tincture or alcohol and water. Shake well before applying. Liniments are also useful when an oil on its own would be too 'hot', for example, to rub the joints in hot-arthritic conditions. Rose*

*oil and chamomile tincture is very soothing and relaxing. Thyme and rosemary infused oil with peppermint tincture and an optional pinch of cayenne or ginger is good for aches and pains, especially after flu.*

**Pessaries and suppositories**
*Pessaries for irritations, thrush and infections can be made by melting together 2g beeswax, 10 ml/2 teaspoons infused herb oil and 15 g/½ oz cocoa butter and pouring the mixture into pessary moulds. Suppositories are made in the same way. A quick method for suppositories involves mixing powdered herb into melted cocoa butter in a ratio of 1 herb : 3 cocoa butter, and pouring into moulds.*

# Ointments

OINTMENTS CONTAIN ONLY OILY INGREDIENTS – *fats or oils*
*thickened with wax. Any wax can be used, including candle*
*wax and paraffin wax, but most herbalists prefer to use*
*beeswax, as it brings extra healing properties of its own to*
*the preparation. Marigold infused oil makes a good,*
*general-purpose ointment: use sunflower or almond oil to*
*make a neutral ointment.*
*The heavy, greasy nature of ointments means that they stay on*
*the skin for a long time, forming a soothing, healing and*
*protective layer. They are especially useful for infants, for old*
*people and for areas of delicate skin, such as the lips and*
*eyelids. They can also be used for very rough, dry skin such as*
*on the feet, knees or elbows.*
*Ointments keep body heat and water in. This makes them*
*valuable for deep aches and rheumatism, which are worse in*
*cold weather. They should not be used in hot, inflamed or*
*weepy skin conditions.*

## Simple ointments

### INGREDIENTS

300 ml/½ pint/1¼ cups home-
made herbal infused oil or
cooking oil
✿
25 g/1 oz yellow beeswax, grated
or thinly chopped

1 If you want to make a different
quantity of ointment to that
described here, the amounts you
need should be in a ratio of 10
quantities of oil to 1 quantity of wax.
Put the oil and beeswax into a
heatproof jug or a pan.

2 Stand the jug or pan in a larger
pan and place on the stove.
Carefully pour water into the larger
pan until the water level is just below
the level of the oil. Bring the water to
a gentle boil and then turn the heat
down. Simmer until the beeswax is
melted, stirring occasionally with a
metal spoon.

**Above:** *The ointment will set with a small dimple in the middle. Melt the reserved ointment, using the water bath as before, and top up the jars to produce a smooth surface. Allow the ointment to cool and put the lids on the jars. Label with the contents, use and date.*

3 Remove the jug or inner pan from the larger pan and allow the molten ointment to cool a little. Pour it into clean jars before it starts to set. Fill the jars to within 1 cm/½ inch of the top, reserving a little of the ointment for topping up later, and leave open until the ointment has set.

# Making perfumed ointments

*Sweet-smelling ointments and infused oils were the original perfumes. The ancient Egyptians were experts at making them and exported them to many countries. They used clarified beef fat boiled in sweet wine as a base. Virgin olive oil thickened with beeswax makes a good substitute.*

*Any sweet-scented flowers, leaves or spices can be used. The Egyptians favoured lilies, broom, marjoram, cinnamon, sweet flag*

*and cardamom. Experiment to find your own favourites. Adding a resin such as myrrh will help the staying power of a perfume. Any resin can be used, but myrrh is traditionally best.*

*Make an infused oil with the spices and resins first, then use this oil to make an infused oil with the fresh flowers, adding beeswax to make an ointment. Smear the ointment on your pulse points to release the perfume.*

# Quick method with powdered herbs

*If infused oils are not available an ointment can be made out of ground herbs or spices mixed with oil and thickened with wax. The herbs must be very finely ground or the end result will be too gritty for more than occasional use. Ground herbs bought for culinary use are generally not fine enough and need to be ground down further. One way of doing this is to use a coffee grinder and then sift the powder through a very fine strainer, though the best way is to use a pestle and mortar – this takes some time, but is good exercise! Finely powdered herbs are obtainable in some specialist herb shops.*

1 Put the oil, chopped beeswax and powdered herb or spice (in this case ginger) into a small pan. Put the lid on and stand it in a large pan. Pour water into the large pan up to the level of the oil in the inner pan. Bring the water to the boil, then reduce the heat and simmer for 1 hour.

2 Allow to cool a little, take out the inner pan and remove the lid. Allow the contents to cool, stirring all the time, so that the powdered herb or spice stays in suspension. Cooling can be hastened by standing the pot in a bowl of cold water.

**INGREDIENTS**

150 ml/¼ pint/⅔ cup cooking oil (olive or sunflower will do, but walnut and almond are more nourishing)
✾
15 g/½ oz beeswax, grated or chopped
✾
50 g/2 oz powdered herb or 25 g/1 oz powdered spice

*Ointments made following the recipe on pages 34–5 can also be used as a base for powdered herb ointments. Simply add 1 part of powdered herb to 4 parts of ointment and heat in a simmering water bath for 1 hour. In this way any ointment can be adapted to suit a particular need. Ginger powder is used for aches and pains, capsicum (sparingly) for unbroken chilblains and post-shingles neuralgia, parsley for soothing bites and stings and marigold for healing and protecting minor cuts.*

*When almost set, ladle the ointment into clean jars, using a palette knife or flexible kitchen knife. Label the jars with the name, use and date. Store in a cool place. These ointments will keep for several months.*

# Plaisters

*Plaisters are an old-fashioned remedy, especially useful for easing deep and persistent aches and pains. They are made by spreading a thick ointment on to a cloth, which is then applied to the skin, covered and left on for 2–3 days. The herbs work deeply and consistently and a plaister feels warm and supportive. This is especially useful for alleviating pain in the limbs and joints which is caused or worsened by cold, damp weather. Because plaisters are made from ointments they should not be used on hot, inflamed and weepy conditions. If plaisters are to be used for a long time, reduce the amount of rubifacient herbs like ginger and cayenne by half.*

*You will need home-made herb ointment or home-made infused oil, beeswax and powdered herb – sage infused oil and ginger powder make a good combination.*

**1** Cut a sufficient length of bandage and lay it on a clean surface. As soon as the ointment starts to set – when it is still at the stage of slightly runny butter – spread it on to the bandage in a thick layer as if you were buttering bread. The plaister may be applied at this stage, or it may be kept for future use.

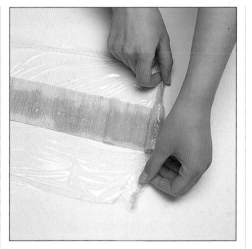

**2** To keep the plaister, cover it with a strip of clingfilm (plastic wrap), with a 2.5 cm/1 inch overlap on each side of the bandage. Turn it over and roll it up, not too tightly. Squeeze the surplus clingfilm (plastic wrap) together to seal up the sides. Store in a clean, dry container such as a tin. Label the container with the name, date and use.

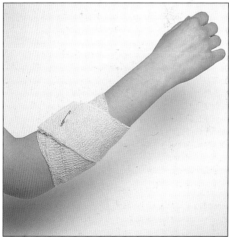

**3** To use the plaister, put the roll into a steamer or a colander over a pan of boiling water. Heat gently for a few minutes until the plaister regains its flexibility. Remove from the heat, remove the clingfilm (plastic wrap) and immediately wrap around the painful limb or joint. Cover with another bandage to hold it firmly in place. Leave on for a day or two and replace as necessary.

# Creams

CREAMS ARE LIGHTER THAN OINTMENTS. *They contain water, or*
*water-based extracts (herbal teas, decoctions and tinctures),*
*as well as oils (oils, fats and waxes). Oil and water do not mix*
*of their own accord, so an emulsifying agent has to be used to*
*combine them. Typical emulsifying agents include egg yolks (as*
*in making mayonnaise), lanolin (also called wool fat and used*
*in many commercial creams) and beeswax. Egg yolk*
*emulsions do not keep well without preservatives, and many*
*people are allergic to lanolin. Beeswax emulsions keep well,*
*are totally natural and bring the added healing potential of the*
*beeswax to a herbal cream.*
*Creams are more cooling than ointments and are more suitable*
*for hot, inflamed and weepy skin conditions. They are also*
*better for warm, damp areas of the body, such as the groin.*
*Beeswax makes a fairly heavy cream which is both cooling*
*and protecting.*

## Simple creams

### INGREDIENTS

**50 ml/2 fl oz/3¹/₂ tablespoons**
**home-made herbal infused oil**

❧

**15 g/¹/₂ oz yellow beeswax,**
**grated or finely cut**

❧

**50 ml/2 fl oz/3¹/₂ tablespoons**
**herbal tea, decoction**
**or tincture**

1 Put the infused oil and beeswax into a small bowl or pan and the herbal tea, decoction or tincture into another small bowl or pan. Stand both bowls in a roasting pan. Fill the roasting pan with water to just below the level of the liquids and put it on the stove. Bring the water to the boil, turn the heat down and wait for the beeswax to melt.

2 Remove the roasting pan from the heat and allow it to cool a little. Pick up the bowl containing the herbal tea, using a folded cloth or oven glove, and pour it slowly into the oil, beating all the time with a hand-held electric food mixer. It is important to pour very slowly, only a few drops at a time, and to set the food mixer at its slowest speed.

**Above:** *Rosemary hair finisher brushed in regularly gives gloriously lustrous hair. For a healthy scalp, massage a small amount well in 20 minutes before washing the hair, then wash normally. No extra conditioner is needed. To make the hair finisher, take 30 g/1 oz fresh rosemary and 150 ml/5 fl oz coconut oil. Infuse over a bain marie for 2 hours, then strain. It can be made stronger by repeating up to 3 times with fresh rosemary.*

**3** Pour the cream into clean jars. When set, put the lids on the jars, label them with the name, date and use and store in a cool place. Creams do not keep as well as ointments, but beeswax creams will last for a few months. Creams made with tinctures will keep longer than those made with teas and decoctions, since they have the preserving power of the alcohol.

## Other useful oils

*Coconut oil (sometimes called butter) is a soft, white vegetable oil which is semi-solid at room temperature, yet melts in response to slight heat. For example, it melts instantly on contact with the skin, allowing preparations to be spread exceedingly thinly and absorbed.*

*Cocoa butter is a creamy yellow oil which is totally solid at room temperature. It is harder than coconut and melts much more slowly. This is useful in suppositories, pessaries and plaisters when slow release is important. Suppositories will take between ½–4 hours to melt, depending on the recipe.*

*The unique qualities of coconut oil and cocoa butter make them very useful additions to the herbal pharmacy. Both can be used in the same way as all other fats, for infusions or mixed into ointments and creams.*

# Syrups and Honeys

HERBAL SYRUPS AND HONEYS *are nutritive and pleasant to take.*
*You can make syrups from all herbs and spices but it is not*
*always appropriate to do so because bitterness is an important*
*part of some herbs, stimulating the appetite and a sluggish*
*digestive reflex. Syrups are best made to give soothing,*
*antiseptic, demulcent and nutritive qualities. They are*
*especially useful to ease a tight chest and sore throat. Whether*
*taken internally or applied externally, they are both*
*soothing and healing.*
*Honey is easily digested and gives fast energy. This is useful*
*to the old, weak or convalescent, but it should not be taken by*
*the diabetic or sugar intolerant. The recipe and method below*
*is the same for all herbs and spices.*

## Herbal syrup

*This method of making syrup can be used for most herbs. Thyme is a good one to try first, as it is an excellent standby as an antiseptic expectorant and a base for many cough syrups. If it is well made the syrup can be kept for over a year. In a very hot climate it is safer to keep syrup in the refrigerator, otherwise it may ferment.*

---

**INGREDIENTS**

**40 g/1½ oz chopped herb**

✿

**900 ml/1½ pints/3¾ cups water**

✿

**450 g/1 lb sugar or honey**

---

**DOSE:**

**Adult: 2–3 teaspoons 3–6 times daily**

**Child: 1 teaspoon 3–6 times daily**

**1** Put the chopped herbs and the water into a pan and bring to the boil. Cover with a tight-fitting lid, turn the heat down low and simmer gently for 20 minutes.

**2** Allow the liquid to cool a little and strain into a measuring jug or another pan. Press the herb with a spoon in order to extract all the goodness. Discard the boiled herbs and keep the liquid.

**3** Return the liquid to the heat and simmer very gently, uncovered, until reduced to 200 ml/7 fl oz/⅞ cup. The slower the reduction the better. The reduced liquid is a decoction.

**4** Add the sugar or honey to the pan. Dissolve slowly and simmer for a few minutes, stirring all the time, until you reach a syrupy consistency. Let the mixture bubble for a moment, but do not overheat as it will turn into a caramel toffee instead.

*Pour the syrup into clean bottles and label them with the name, the date and the dose.*

# Fresh onion syrup

*Onion syrup can be used to help fight off colds. It will keep for up to a week in a cool place or in the refrigerator. You can use any type of onion to make this syrup, although red onions have an extra-mild demulcency which is good for children.*

## INGREDIENTS

**1 large or 2 small onions**

**450 g/1 lb brown granulated sugar or clear honey**

## DOSE

**Adult: 2 teaspoons 3 times daily or up to every 2 hours to help fight off a cold**

**Child: ½–1 teaspoon 3–6 times daily.**

1 Peel and slice the onion.

2 Put 5 cm/2 inches of onion in the bottom of a jam jar and cover with 5 cm/2 inches of sugar or honey. Fill the jar with alternate layers of onion and sugar or honey, pressing each layer down firmly before adding the next.

3 Cover the last layer of onion with a thick sugar or honey layer, and leave overnight. If sugar has been used, most of it will have liquefied into a syrup by dissolving into the onion juice – this is the onion syrup.

4 In the morning, strain off the liquid and throw away any undissolved sugar left at the bottom of the jar. Pour into bottles, label them with the name, date and dose and store in a cool, dark place. It will keep for up to a week in a cool place or in the refrigerator.

# Garlic honey

*Garlic is antibiotic and honey is antiseptic. Together they make a daily preventative tonic, a strengthening restorative or a remedial treatment.*

*Garlic honey is a basic, multi-purpose cure-all which should be a standby in every household. Select healthy, bursting bulbs of garlic, preferably organic.*

*However garlic is taken, it leaves the body by being exhaled via the lungs. The lungs are disinfected during this process and the scent of garlic on the breath is proof of its efficiency.*

---

**INGREDIENTS**

**2 whole heads of garlic**

❀

**450 g/1 lb honey**

---

## DOSE

**As a tonic or preventative:** ½ **teaspoon daily**

**As a remedy:** ½ **teaspoon 3 times daily, or 6 times in acute conditions**

**Take directly, or add to lemon and water, diluted herb vinegar drinks or milks**

**Apply directly to the skin for bites, grazes and wounds**

**Dilute 1 teaspoon in 120 ml/ 4 fl oz/½ cup water as a skin lotion**

**Dilute 1 teaspoon in 600 ml/ 1 pint/2½ cups water for a douche**

**For infants, rub garlic honey on to the soles of the feet**

1 Peel the garlic heads, slice off the bases of the cloves and crush them in a garlic press.

2 Put the crushed garlic into a pestle and mortar and pound until they become partially transparent. (In the living plant, the active compounds are stored separately. Crushing releases and mixes them.)

3 Add 2 tablespoons of honey to the garlic and continue pounding. Pound until the garlic is totally transparent. Add the remaining honey and mix it in well.

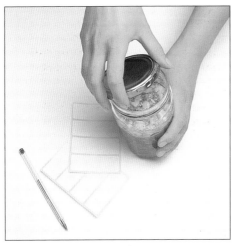

4 Pour the garlic honey into a bottle and label it with the name, date and dose.

43

# Skin and Body Care

THE SKIN IS A COMPLICATED ORGAN. *It is our first line of defence against infection; its millions of nerve endings provide our sense of touch; it has to be strong yet flexible and sensitive, and capable of excreting oils and waste products. It remains soft by continually renewing itself and by self-lubrication. A healthy skin has a slightly acid pH balance and secretes anti-microbial substances which help to maintain a balance of friendly micro-organisms. It is impossible to have a healthy skin without internal health; many skin problems arise from a deeper underlying cause.*

*There are many 'natural' skin-care products on the market, but making your own ensures that the products are pure and there are no additives or preservatives that may irritate your skin. Always buy the best quality ingredients you can afford.*

## Oat bath

*This oat bath is good for delicate, sensitive skins and for irritable and inflamed skin conditions. Oats soften the water and cleanse the skin. The cloth is reusable. An oat bag can be made for use in a shower – suspend it from the showerhead.*

### INGREDIENTS

**For the bag:**
**a square of loose-weave, natural, unbleached cotton cloth or muslin (cheesecloth) measuring about 45 × 45 cm/18 × 18 inches**
❋
**60 cm/2 ft of ribbon**
❋
**For the filling:**
**75 g/3 oz/1 cup oats**
❋
**2 teaspoons favourite herb or 2 dessertspoons decoction or tincture**

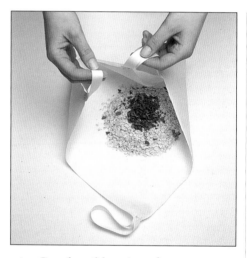

1 Cut the ribbon into four pieces and sew a loop on to each corner of the square of cotton (the length of the loops will depend upon the particular design of your bathtaps, so try them for size). Mix the filling ingredients together, put them into the middle of the cloth and gather the loops together.

2 Hang the loops of the cloth bag over the bathtaps so that the water can run freely through the bag, filling the bath with softened and fragrant water. Other herbs can be added to the bag in order to give a different fragrance or to make a therapeutic soak.

**3** Once the bath has been drawn, the oats and herb mixture in the bag will be soft and milky. Hold the ribbon loops together tightly, squeeze the oats down to the bottom of the bag and knot the loops loosely or tie a string around the neck to make a closed bag. As you squeeze the bag, the oat milk will seep through the pores of the cloth.

**4** Use the bag like a sponge, rubbing it over the body, washing the skin with the milky oat-liquid that seeps through the pores of the cloth. Use plenty of water to keep the bag soft and the oats damp and creamy. This leaves the skin silky smooth. When you have finished, throw away the oats and wash the cloth ready for next time.

# Robbie's gritty oat wash

*This oat wash makes a deep, exfoliating cleanser suitable for removing layers of dry skin and ingrained dirt.*

**INGREDIENTS**

**4 dessertspoons oats**
🌸
**1 teaspoon ground rice**
🌸
**1 teaspoon fine sea salt**
🌸
**1 dessertspoon vegetable oil or home-made infused oil**

*1 Rub the oats through your fingers until the required texture is reached – the rougher the oats, the coarser the eventual wash. Add the rest of the dry ingredients and the oil. Rub well until all the oil has been taken into the mixture. Press down firmly into a clean jar.*

*2 To use, take a small amount of the oat wash on to the palm of one hand and blend it gently with a little water until you have a creamy mixture. Rub the mixture into the skin, using small circular movements and plenty of water. Rinse well and pat dry.*

# Oat and wheat bran rub

*This makes a stimulating body brush! Choose the home-made infused oil according to need: rosemary will stimulate the circulation, thyme will help to break down cellulite and parsley will help with water retention.*

**INGREDIENTS**
**Makes 1 application**

2 tablespoons oats
❀
2 tablespoons wheat bran
❀
2 teaspoons fine salt
❀
2 teaspoons home-made infused oil

*Blend all the ingredients together thoroughly. To use, take a handful of the mixture in the hand or on a dry cloth and rub into the skin using a circular motion. Brush off. This will remove dead skin and stimulate circulation and drainage of the lymph glands, bringing a healthy glow to the skin and helping to rid the body of toxins.*

# Hand bath

*Herbalist Maurice Messague has examined the medicinal efficiency of hand and foot baths, and advocates them as a major therapeutic strategy. Use any herb for a bath. Soak the limb for 20 minutes; the whole body relaxes while the herb is absorbed – simple, beautiful and efficient.*

# Simple lemon hand lotion

*This simple, nourishing and moisturizing skin lotion depends on the quality of the ingredients. A good oil makes a fine lotion. Wheatgerm is nourishing, almond and peach kernel are moisturizing, walnut is protective and sealing. The lotion is slightly sticky, so it is best used at bedtime. It also makes a sound protective base under makeup or powder.*

**INGREDIENTS**

2 teaspoons lemon juice
❀
2 teaspoons walnut oil or home-made infused oil

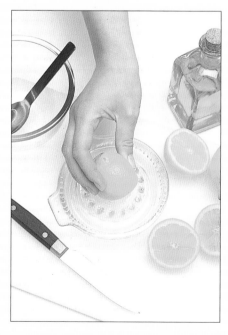

*Mix the lemon juice and oil very well until creamy. Apply immediately, rubbing well in.*

# Peter's mustard foot bath

*After a long walk in which the feet feel flat and hot, or when cold seems to eat into the bones around the ankles, a foot bath relieves and revitalizes the whole body.*

**INGREDIENTS**

**2 teaspoons ground mustard powder**

**2.2 litres/4 pints/10 cups hot water**

*Mix the mustard and water together. Soak the feet for 20 minutes. Relax, close your eyes and allow the warmth to spread up your legs through your body. Dry well and keep the feet warm afterwards.*

# Richard's thyme foot talc

**INGREDIENTS**

**1 tablespoon cornflour (cornstarch)**

**or**

**1 tablespoon maize flour**

**1 teaspoon bicarbonate of soda**

**1 teaspoon finely powdered thyme**

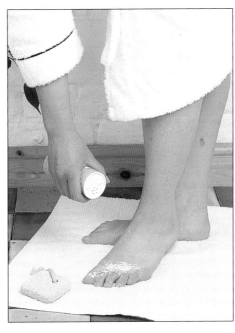

*Grind the ingredients together into a fine powder. For athlete's foot, rub the skin, especially between the toes, with lemon peel, releasing the oil, and then dust with a fine sprinkling of the foot powder. Parsley foot talc is good for feet which become over-hot and tired.*

# Eye care

*Eyes become tired, irritated and dry as they cope with the dust, smoke and pollution of our cities and the pollens and chemical sprays of the countryside.*

*This soothing eye bath is simple to make and effective. Fennel seed, chamomile and parsley infusions also make good eye baths.*

**INGREDIENTS**

**½ teaspoon sea salt**

**120 ml/4 fl oz/½ cup distilled water**

*Dissolve the salt completely in the water. Use the solution to bathe and rinse your eyes.*

### Revitalizing the eyes

*Are you tired, or having trouble focusing? Is tension behind the eyes moving into a headache? Do not throw tea bags away – put them in the refrigerator. At the end of the day, close your eyes, rest your head and neck and place the cold teabags over your eyes. Cold chamomile calms irritations and allergic reactions, parsley and tea clear and tone red eyes. Slices of cucumber can also revitalize eyes in seconds.*

# Herbs Around the Home

HEALTH STARTS WITH WHOLESOME FOOD *and a wholesome environment. In earlier times, herbs were added in their handfuls to soups and broths. Herb butter, cheese and salt all graced the table and strengthened the body. Hygiene and comfort are also important aspects of health care. In the early medical books there was little differentiation; care for the self, for others and for the home all contributed to an overall sense of well-being and harmony with the environment. All that nature provided was used, everything having value and worth. The produce of the garden contributed cleansers, bleaches, conditioners and cut flowers for bedrooms, pillows and sweet linen bags, in addition to the more obvious remedies.*

## Herb bags

*Pot pourris kept the house fresh and herb pillows or small bags were popular, restful sleep and sweet dreams being essential for well-being. Herb bags were used for other purposes too – this recipe is called 'the moth destroyer'.*

### INGREDIENTS

**15 g/½ oz cloves**

✳

**10 cardamom pods**

✳

**1 teaspoon salt**

✳

**15 g/½ oz peppermint**

✳

**15 g/½ oz rosemary**

✳

**dried peel of 1 lemon**

*Crush the cloves, cardamom and salt to a fine powder. Blend with the herbs and put in bags. Alternatively, grind everything into a fine powder and sprinkle it generously over your clothes.*

# Pomanders

Pomanders hold their fragrance for many years, even decades. The most common form is an orange speared with cloves, although lemons and any aromatic seed such as fennel, cumin and caraway can also be used.

Make small, shallow holes in the peel, not deep enough to pierce the flesh. Put cloves in the holes, in rows and patches or at random. Finish by rubbing with ground cloves and salt. Hang up and allow to dry naturally.

# Smudge sticks

*Smudge sticks are used to freshen the air, clear unpleasant smells and warm the atmosphere.*
*Used sparingly, they bring the fresh fragrances of the forest and garden into the house.*

**1** Pick sprigs of fresh, healthy herbs such as sage, thyme, rosemary, fennel leaves and stalks, pine or cypress. Supermarket herbs growing in small pots are large enough to make useful small sticks.

**2** Hold the sprigs together in a tight bundle and tie with cotton thread. It is important to use cotton as synthetic threads smoulder and fall apart. Wrap the thread around the bundle to hold all the leaves in, then tie securely every 1 cm/½ inch. Leave the sticks to dry naturally over the course of a few weeks.

**3** To use, hold the end about 5 cm/ 2 inches above a candle flame. It will take time but the end will become red and smoulder, releasing a thin trail of fragrant smoke. Some oily herbs may splutter and spit oil as they burn. When the smudge stick has done its work, put it out carefully and trim the end ready for next time.

# Medical fumigation

*Steam inhalations clear the sinuses; smoke inhalations relax and soothe the chest muscles. This is useful in a tight chest, night wheezes and asthma, especially for young children. Breathe in a relaxed rhythm, letting the in-breath take in the smoke and the out-breath fan the embers. It is not necessary to stand over the herbs. They are safe for children if burnt nearby.*

### INGREDIENTS

**1 part fennel seed**

❀

**1 part aniseed**

❀

**3 parts sage**

**1** *Crush the fennel seed and aniseed and rub into the sage.*

**2** *Put a small heap of the mixture on to a smouldering charcoal block of the type sold for burning incense. The herbs can also be sprinkled on to a fire, hot coals or a barbecue.*

**50**

# Smoking

*Smoking mixtures have a long tradition in European and American herbal medicine. Dried herbs need to be cured with honey or they are raw and dry on the throat. Sage is used as the base herb because it burns well and others are added to give taste. Rosemary, thyme, basil, bay, parsley, tarragon and aniseed or fennel powder each add distinction. In his* Natural History *(AD77), the Roman writer Pliny recommends 'smoke drawn into the mouth through a reed and swallowed . . . a remedy for an obstinate cough'. Good smoke clears the brain and relaxes the chest.*

1 Mix the honey and water together. Rub the herbs well together and add the honeyed water a teaspoon at a time. Rub well into the leaves until they are slightly damp.

2 Lay out on a shallow dish for a few days, so that the water can slowly evaporate. Turn from time to time. When the mixture is dry enough to burn but not yet bone dry, place in an airtight tin, label and date.

---

### INGREDIENTS

**1 teaspoon honey**

❧

**4 teaspoons water**

❧

**15 g/½ oz sage**

❧

**2 teaspoons of any other herbs**

---

*The mixture can be rolled into cigarettes, or alternatively burnt on a charcoal block and the smoke inhaled either simply by standing over it or through a tube of paper.*

# Herb butter

*Herb butter brings the piquant flavour of herbs to any baking or frying. The smell of melting herb butter on freshly baked bread is the evocative scent of home. A curl will enrich a plain soup and aid digestion. You will find that a dollop of herb butter in 120 ml/ 4 fl oz/½ cup of hot water makes a useful alternative to herb honey for children who do not like honey. Or spread a sliced stick of French bread with plenty of herb butter and leave it in the oven to melt through to create a delicious herb accompaniment to any meal.*

## INGREDIENTS

**100 g/4 oz/½ cup best unsalted butter**

❈

**1 teaspoon finely chopped herbs (fresh or dried)**

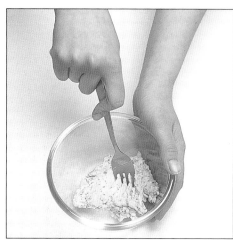

**1** Soften and mash the butter, add the herbs and blend together so that the herbs are spread evenly in the butter. Pat into a block and put in the refrigerator to cool and rest.

**Below:** *Once made, herb butter can easily be moulded into attractive shapes such as balls, cubes or beautiful butter curls.*

# Herb salt

*Any herb or combination of herbs can be used – experiment to find a favourite. Garlic, onion, celery seed, parsley, cardamom and caraway seeds are good to start with.*

---

### INGREDIENTS

**2 teaspoons finely chopped fresh herb or herbs**

✳

**350 g/12 oz/1 cup best sea salt**

---

*'The use of Sage in the month of May, with butter, Parsley and some salt, is very frequent in our Country to continue health to the body . . . [Use] Rosemary and other good hearbes for the same purpose.'*

John Parkinson, *Theatrum Botanicum*, 1604

**1** Grind the herbs and salt together and press down into a jar. The salt can be used immediately but it is best after standing for a week.

# Herb cheese

*Leaves from a variety of herbs are used in many rural areas to wrap cheese, which imparts extra flavour to the cheese. Proper herb cheeses, however, are made by mixing the herb juice with rennet and adding it to the milk, then skimming and pressing the rising curd.*

*Simple herb dips and spreads can easily be made by adding chopped herbs to soured cream, soya cheese, cream cheese or yogurt. Leave these in the refrigerator for a few hours before using to let the flavour of the herb spread throughout the dip or spread.*

# INGREDIENTS

*'Are you going to Scarborough Fair
(Parsley, sage, rosemary and thyme)
Remember me to one who lives there –
She once was a true love of mine.'*

*Plants and people have a long history together, a history celebrated in story and song as well as in the kitchen and still room. Some of the story can be found in this section, along with recipes and tips. Try the recipes, adapt them for your family and add to the story yourself.*

# Some Useful Ingredients

Below is a list of all the useful herbs, spices, vegetables and condiments commonly found in shops, showing their basic properties. Sometimes these properties seem contradictory. This is because natural substances are a complex mixture of compounds and these compounds have a variety of actions which balance, buffer, enhance or synergistically work together in a general healing strategy, unlike the single 'magic bullet' approach of drugs. This is one of the major tenets of herbal medicine and natural healing: the whole herb, fruit, seed or vegetable is a better medicine than an isolated extract – for example, lemon juice is a better remedy than citric acid. While reading this list, try to balance the properties with a picture of the overall character of the plant. See page 94 for a glossary of the terms used.

Ingredients that are described in detail in the following pages are marked with an asterisk.

## Spices

**ANISEED\*** Antiseptic, antispasmodic and warming digestive. Relaxes stomach and chest, especially in all children's ailments.

**CARAWAY** Warming, antispasmodic and digestive.

**CARDAMOM\*** Aromatic. A warming, balancing digestive. Tonic; raises the spirits and clears the mind. Expectorant.

**CAYENNE\*** Hot, stimulating, antiseptic, antispasmodic, rubifacient. Improves circulation and adds heat to other remedies.

**CINNAMON\*** Circulatory stimulant, warming digestive. Astringent for clearing nose and lungs.

**CLOVES\*** Warming, antiseptic, germicide, carminative, expectorant, anaesthetic.

**CORIANDER** Gentle warming antispasmodic and carminative.

**CORN SILK\*** Soothing diuretic.

**FENNEL SEEDS\*** Warming carminative, balances digestion. Diuretic. Stimulates milk flow. Not to be used in pregnancy.

**GINGER\*** Stimulating, antispasmodic, relaxant, diaphoretic, digestive. Relieves nausea. Warms the whole system.

**JUNIPER BERRIES\*** Antiseptic diuretic. Not to be used in pregnancy.

**MUSTARD SEED** Warming antispasmodic. Rubifacient. Emetic.

**NUTMEG** Antiseptic, analgesic, digestive stimulant. Relaxing in small doses; emetic in large doses.

**TURMERIC** Antiseptic, aromatic digestive, hepatic.

## Herbs

**BASIL** Warming digestive. Nerve stimulant and tonic. Helps reduce stress and clear the mind. Aphrodisiac.

**BAY** Warming digestive. Locally warming and anaesthetic.

**CHAMOMILE\*** Anti-inflammatory, antiseptic, anti-allergy. Slightly bitter digestive. Relaxant and sedative. Febrifuge for children. For children's ailments in general.

**HORSERADISH** Warming, antiseptic, antispasmodic, diaphoretic, decongestant.

**MARJORAM** Antiseptic, tonic digestive, antidepressant. Slightly expectorant.

**MARIGOLD\*** Antiseptic, anti-fungal. Strengthens the immune system.

**PARSLEY\*** Antiseptic diuretic. Cleanser. Tonic for women in general. Not to be taken in pregnancy.

**PEPPERMINT\*** Warming carminative. Digestive, antiseptic, anti-spasmodic. Cooling on the skin.

**ROSEMARY\*** Warming digestive. Circulatory stimulant. Hepatic. Tonic.

**SAGE\*** Antiseptic astringent. Tonic and restorative. Febrifuge. Balances female hormones. Not to be used in pregnancy.

**THYME\*** Antiseptic, bactericide, carminative, expectorant.

## Other Ingredients

**BARLEY\*** Cooling, nutritive, soothing and healing.

**CABBAGE\*** Cooling and nutritive. Anti-inflammatory, detoxifying, antiseptic.

**CARROT\*** Soothing and nutritive, very easily digested. Diuretic.

**CUCUMBER\*** Soothing, cooling, anti-inflammatory. Diuretic.

**FIGS\*** Nourishing and laxative. Strengthening to the lungs.

**GARLIC AND ONION\*** Strongly antiseptic, anti-fungal, anti-viral and bactericide. Decongestant expectorant. Depurative. Balances circulation and helps lower blood pressure.

**LEMON\*** Cooling. Antiseptic. Soothing, healing, anti-bacterial, anti-fungal. Detoxifying diuretic.

**LETTUCE** A bitter digestive. Cooling and sedative.

**OATS\*** Soothing, nutritive and strengthening. Nerve tonic. Drawing.

**HONEY\*** Nutritive, antiseptic, soothing, demulcent, expectorant.

**OILS\*** Warming. Soothing and lubricating laxatives.

**SALT\*** Antiseptic. Stimulates the appetite.

**VINEGAR\*** Cooling, antiseptic, anti-fungal. Clearing and cleansing.

**WINES, SPIRITS, BEERS\*** Stimulant. Relaxant. Warming to the digestion. Externally cooling and drying.

## *Allium sativum and A. cepa*
# Garlic and Onion

Garlic is a hardy perennial with long, thin leaves and decorative flowers. The bulb consists of several bulblets, or cloves, enclosed in a white membrane. Garlic is antiseptic, anti-pathogenic (anti-bacterial, anti-fungal, anti-parasitic, anti-viral), slightly demulcent, expectorant, anti-allergic, a circulatory stimulant . . . the list of properties could be even longer. Culpeper accounts it 'the poor man's treacle, it being a remedy for all diseases and hurts'. Modern herbalist Simon Mills says, 'Such are the virtues claimed for garlic that it might all be thought too good to be true, if most of them were not being independently supported by research.'

Garlic originated in Central Asia, and seems to have been used from time immemorial to prevent contagion and heal infections. It is now popular worldwide, and in countries where typhus and cholera are endemic nearly everyone adds small amounts of it to food as a preventative.

Some early herbalists rejected garlic on account of what Culpeper termed its 'strong and offensive smell', but the smell is part of its therapeutic action as a chest antiseptic and its virtues are such that its odour is now accepted. There are many forms of garlic available – pearls, tablets and liquid – but fresh is still best. Roasting it makes it easily digestible, while eating garlic butter and garlic bread is a good way of obtaining a

### NEAL'S MEDICINAL MILK

*This remedy is suitable for small children. It is calming, soothing, demulcent, warming, nutritive, expectorant and antiseptic. Milk is used here as a nutritive medicine, rather than as an everyday drink. Some children are intolerant of cow's milk, in which case use a vegetable substitute such as soya or nut milk.*

*1 small onion, sliced*
*600 ml/1 pint/2½ cups milk*
*a pinch of spice (optional)*

*Put the onion and milk into a pan and heat slowly until the liquid reaches simmering point. Cover the pan and simmer for 20 minutes. Strain before using. This remedy will keep in the refrigerator for a few days.*

*To use: For newborn babies, the mother should drink it freely if she is breast feeding. Otherwise, rub it on to the baby's chest and feet daily; for children over six months, 1 teaspoon 3–6 times a day; children over seven may drink it freely.*

### ONION POULTICE

*Roast a whole onion until it is soft. Cut in half and apply to the affected area. This is useful for drawing splinters, cleaning wounds and alleviating earache.*

### GARLIC AND CABBAGE WATER

*This is a good remedy for those who find garlic too hot to take by itself.*

*¼ head cabbage, chopped*
*4 garlic cloves, chopped*
*1.2 litres/2 pints/5 cups water*
*honey to taste*

*Put the cabbage, garlic and water into a pan, heat until simmering point is reached and then simmer for 10 minutes. Strain and add honey to taste.*
*To use: adults may drink this freely.*

daily intake. A large quantity of parsley eaten with the garlic minimizes the smell.

Garlic thins the blood, so that less pressure is needed to pump it around the body and it is less prone to clotting. It also lowers cholesterol levels and blood sugar. It is the prime remedy for chest infections, used both internally and externally.

Onion has similar properties to garlic in a wetter, more soothing and demulcent form. It is more suitable for children, old people and those with a hot constitution and can be used as a daily remedy to maintain health. Onion juice is used for wounds, spots, styes and ear infections. According to a 17th-century manuscript of collected recipes, 'The juice taketh away the heat or scalding with water or oil, as also burning with fire and gunpowder, as is set forth by a very skilful Surgeon Mr. William Clowes one of the Queen's Surgeons.'

Some people find garlic and onion too hard on their stomach. Leek is in the same family as garlic and shares many of the virtues, but in a milder form. The Welsh herbal tradition extols the virtues of leek soup to combat weakness caused by cold damp weather and for chronic cough and pneumonia.

*Avena sativa*

# Oats

There is a TV commercial for porridge oats which shows a small boy trudging through the snow. The elements do not bother him as he is surrounded by a protective aura bestowed by the porridge he has eaten for breakfast. This is an accurate image of oats. They are soothing, nutritious, sustaining and protecting; they strengthen mind, body and spirit, and they form an ideal foundation in childhood, building strong bones and teeth.

Oats are easily digested and are restorative after illness, combating general debility. They contain silica, which aids healing, and minerals including potassium and magnesium. It has been shown that eating oats lowers blood cholesterol levels and thus helps to protect against heart attacks. Oat bran is softer than wheat bran and more easily tolerated by people with constipation or irritable bowels.

Oats make an excellent skin cleaner with a balanced pH for sensitive skins or when skin conditions like eczema make it impossible to use manufactured creams and soaps.

## HOT OAT COMPRESS

*Oats make a good base for hot compresses and fomentations as they retain heat and have a gentle drawing action. This mixture makes 1½ tablespoons of compress.*

*1 tablespoon porridge oats*
*60 ml/4 tablespoons water, herb tea or diluted tincture*
*1 teaspoon finely chopped fresh or dried herb (optional)*

*Put all the ingredients in a pan, bring to the boil over a very low heat and stir until the mixture thickens and the water has been absorbed. Take off the heat and allow to stand for 5 minutes. This is now ready to use. Reheat, let the mixture cool to the required temperature and apply in a thick layer. Cover with clingfilm (plastic wrap) and bandage into place. Plain oats can be used or herbs can be added: chamomile acts as a calming antiseptic for skin irritations and inflammations, parsley is effective for arthritic pains and boils, and garlic and onion are good for infections.*

## OAT TONIC

*This is a calming, nourishing, strengthening restorative, ideal for sickly children, the elderly or convalescents. It restores digestive balance after taking antibiotics, undergoing surgery or suffering from gastritis or any poisoning.*

*350 ml/12 fl oz/1½ cups cold boiled water*
*75 g/3 oz/1 cup flaked or rolled oats*
*½ teaspoon ground ginger or allspice*
*juice of ½ lemon*
*5 ml/1 teaspoon honey*

*Pour the water over the oats and spice and leave to stand for 30 minutes. In the morning strain through a cloth and wring out the juice. Add the lemon and honey to the juice, mix well and bottle. This tonic will keep in the refrigerator for several days.*
*To use: take 1 teaspoon 2–3 times a day until finished.*

## OAT WASH

*Makes 25 ml/1 fl oz*
*6 teaspoons porridge oats*
*1 teaspoon vegetable oil such as sunflower*
*2 drops lavender essential oil (optional)*

*Rub the oats to a fine powder and blend the oil in well. Press this mixture into a small jar.*
*To use: Take a small amount of the mixture in your hand and work in a little water until you have a paste. Rub into your skin and rinse off with plenty of water. For a purifying mask: Smear the paste on to your skin and leave on for 20 minutes. Rinse well and pat dry.*

Porridge makes a good start to the day; if you tire of making it with milk and sugar, or the traditional Scottish salt and water, fruit juice is a good alternative. Cook the oats in the juice, or soak overnight and eat raw. Apple juice with a pinch of allspice is warming, orange and caraway is tangy, prune and ginger is comforting. A good pinch of powdered ginger or cinnamon will prolong the warming effect, while a small pinch of nutmeg will lift the spirits. Serve with dried fruit to give day-long energy.

Oat straw and unprocessed oat grains have the same soothing, strengthening and tonic properties. They can be used in decoctions and tinctures.

*Brassica oleracea*

# Cabbage

When humans were still hunter-gatherers, the plants they used were picked from the woods. Once they became farmers plants were cultivated, but only valuable and useful ones were worth the effort needed with the simple tools available. Was cabbage really that valuable? Experience, and modern research, answers yes!

Cabbage is a rich store of vitamins and minerals, especially calcium and iron. Deficiency diseases are rare in people who eat salads and greens as a regular part of

## PICKLED RED CABBAGE

*1 head of red cabbage, sliced thinly*
*1 teaspoon caraway seeds*
*equal parts of cider vinegar and water,*
*sufficient to cover*

*Put all the ingredients in a pan and simmer gently until the cabbage is soft. Eat hot or cold. Other spices can be added. Interesting additions include orange juice, lemon juice, raisins, chopped apple, cayenne and nuts.*

## CABBAGE POULTICE

*This is wonderful for sore throats and hot, swollen joints.*

*Lightly crush the leaves, blanch in boiling water and wrap around the area. Leave on for 2–4 hours. Renew as necessary.*

## TINA'S SLIMMING TONIC

*2 sweet apples*
*equal amount of white cabbage (about ½ head)*
*1 teaspoon caraway seeds*

*COLD METHOD: If you have a juicer, express the juice of the apples and cabbage. Use the caraway to make 420 ml/⁵⁄₄ pint/1¾ cups tea and add this to the juice.*

*HOT METHOD: Chop the fruit and cabbage into small pieces and add the caraway seeds. Cover with 900ml/1½ pints/3¾ cups water and bring to the boil. Turn the heat down, put the lid on the pan and simmer for 10 minutes. Strain before using.*

*Take this tonic hot, cold or iced. Drink freely while fasting or resting the digestive tract. A pinch of cayenne pepper may be added to give extra warm depth if feeling cold, and honey may also be added to taste. All fruit and vegetable juices are clearing, slightly laxative and nutritive. Many interesting combinations are possible, so experiment and have fun.*

their diet. However, cabbage is more than just a source of vitamins and minerals – it is also cooling, cleansing and detoxifying. It provides dietary fibre and balances acids in the stomach and body.

Cabbage stores very well, and in many parts of the world it is the only vegetable that is available throughout the winter. Sauerkraut (fermented cabbage) maintains its nutritive goodness for longer than the fresh vegetable. In 200BC it was fed to the workmen building the Great Wall of China to help them maintain their strength.

Culpeper, who says that description of cabbage is needless as 'everyone that can write at all may describe them from his own knowledge', lists its properties thus: 'Boiled in broth and eaten opens the body . . . eaten with meat keeps one from surfeiting, and from getting drunk . . . drink and bathe the joints for pain, aches and gouty swellings. Heals all small scabs, pushes, and wheals that break out in the skin . . . for melancholy and windy humours.' Most definitely a valuable plant worth cultivating!

Cabbage water, or a decoction of cabbage, alkalizes the body when it is too acidic, gouty and arthritic. It protects and soothes the guts. Mixed with apple juice or spiced, it makes a soothing and cooling diuretic.

The cabbage family includes many different varieties which have been produced by selective cultivation, including Savoy, kale, Brussels sprouts, cauliflower, broccoli and calabrese. They all share the same excellent nutritive and health-giving properties.

*Calendula officinalis*

# Marigold

Marigold flowers are not generally available in the supermarket, but they are worth searching for. They are so beautiful and useful that you should consider growing some: a window-box full would provide medicine all the year round and, if medicine were not required, they could always be added to soups, salads and stews. The Germans used to add handfuls of pot marigold to their soups and broths to add body, colour and strength. Simply gazing at the clear radiant orange of the flowers is said to strengthen the eyesight. Aemilius Macer, who wrote a treatise on the virtues of herbs which was published throughout the 13th and 14th centuries, says, 'The gold flower is good to be seen, it makes the sight bright and clean.'

Marigold, used both externally and internally, is the single most useful herb for skin conditions of all kinds. Marigold cream, often called calendula cream, is available in many chemists and health food stores and it is easily made. Use it for cuts, abrasions, bruises, spots, fungal conditions and many other types of rash, or as a wash or compress for infected cuts, stings, bites, grazes, inflamed eyes, sore varicose veins and any red, sore-looking skin. The whole plant, but especially the flowers, was used on a large scale by American surgeons to treat wounds sustained during the Civil War, and it received their highest commendation. In her book *Herbal Medicine* (reprinted 1983), Dian Buchman mentions the clinical experiences of Dr Shephard: 'In cases where the skin was broken, I used Calendula [Marigold] as a routine measure and wonderfully quickly it acts. It prevents sepsis [putrefaction]. Why it does it, I do not know; yet the fact remains that it does unless an interfering parent . . . choses to remove the dressing . . . and use his own favorite antiseptic; then we would find that the wound would begin to fester.'

Internally, marigold is strongly antiseptic, anti-fungal and anti inflammatory. It clears the lymphatic system and supports the immune system. Use it as a tea for children's fevers, especially if the neck glands are swollen.

Taken regularly, marigold will clear up cellulite, especially if used in conjunction with massage. Use it as a gargle for sore throats and to relieve the pressure in congested ears. A teaspoon of the tincture in a glass of clean water can be used for the same purposes.

This plant has a particular affinity for women. Taken regularly, marigold tea is helpful for painful periods, tender ovaries and blocked tubes, and maintains equilibrium during the menopause.

When growing or picking marigolds, make sure the plants are *Calendula officinalis* and not *Tagetes* species. French, African and Mexican marigolds are species of *Tagetes*. They have different properties and must not be used for herbal teas.

---

## MARIGOLD PUDDING

*'Take a pretty quantity of marygold flowers very well shred, mingle with a pint of cream on new milk and almost a pound of beef suet chopt very small, the gratings of a twopenny loaf and stirring all together put it into a bag flower'd and tie it fast. It will be boil'd within an hour – or bake it in a pan.'*

Acetaria, John Evelyn (1699)

---

## MARIGOLD AND SAGE DECOCTION

*15 g/½ oz marigold flowers*
*15 g/½ oz sage leaves*
*600 ml/1 pint/2½ cups water*

*Simmer all the ingredients together in a tightly closed pan for 10 minutes. Strain through a sieve (strainer), pressing the herbs to extract all the liquid. Stored in a cool dark place, this decoction will keep for 4–5 days. Drink 120 ml/4 fl oz/½ cup, hot or cold, every 4 hours at the onset of fevers. It also makes an excellent gargle for sore throats. Add the whole 600 ml/1 pint/2½ cups to a bath for itchy genital rashes.*

**CAUTION:** OMIT THE SAGE DURING PREGNANCY

*Capsicum minimum*

# Cayenne

There many different varieties of capsicums, ranging from mild and sweet bell peppers to small fiery bundles of absolute heat. Cayenne is one of the hottest.

Not unexpectedly, it is a hot stimulant. It radiates throughout the whole body, equalizing body temperature from the core to the skin, regulating blood flow and strengthening the heart. It warms cold hands and feet and relaxes tense muscles. In medieval herbal astrology, cayenne is assigned to the sun. Its effect is like having a small internal star glowing in your centre. Imagine lying on warm sand, letting the sun soak through the skin into the long bones of the arms and legs, relaxing and equalizing. This is the action of cayenne.

People talk of the 'spice of life'. What spice do they mean? Carminative cloves? Anti-spasmodic ginger? Relaxing aniseed or fennel? The best candidate is cayenne, as one tiny pinch spices up the whole system. It is an optional

*Remedies break down into hot, cold or neutral; warming and encouraging circulation, cooling and limiting circulation, or keeping everything as it is! The sympathetic practice of hot and cold will nearly always help the body and is a useful strategy when you are unsure of what to do. If too cold, chilled, stiff and slow to heal, or unevenly cold, with areas like the knees being cold and stiff with arthritis, then use warming remedies such as cayenne. If too hot, feverish or just congested with stagnant heat, use cooling remedies such as cucumber.*

## NON'S HOT OIL

*A warming anti-spasmodic for muscle aches, cramps, spasm and chilblains. It improves circulation, warms cold areas and cold joints, and banishes chills from the bones. Once made, this oil becomes so useful and popular around the house that it is impossible to consider life without it.*

*25 g/1 oz cayenne pepper*
*2 tablespoons mustard powder*
*5 cm/2 inches ginger root or 1 tablespoon dried ginger*
*2 teaspoons ground black pepper*
*300 ml/½ pint/1¼ cups vegetable oil*

*Combine the ingredients as described on page 30 to make an infused oil.*

## CAYENNE MOUTHWASH

*Throughout this book many recipes suggest the optional addition of a pinch of cayenne, especially in mouthwashes and gargles. This gives them a warm, antiseptic and penetrative edge. In this recipe the cayenne is not optional – it is an integral part of the remedy, giving a powerful warming sensation, clearing the head and the sinuses.*

*8 g/¼ oz parsley*
*8 g/¼ oz sage*
*1 heaped tablespoon cayenne pepper*
*10 cloves (optional)*
*½ teaspoon ground nutmeg (optional)*
*500ml/18 fl oz/2¼ cups cider vinegar*

*Macerate the ingredients together for 2 weeks, then strain and bottle. Dilute 1 teaspoon with water to use.*

ingredient in many recipes. A pinch will make anything, even porridge oats, warmer and more penetrating. A pinch in herbal teas facilitates the action of the herbs, circulating their healing powers freely throughout the body.

In the physiomedical or botanical tradition of herbalists of the nineteenth century, cayenne was regarded as a major stimulant. Using its action, in small and large doses, to induce activity and aid elimination was a classic physiomedical strategy.

Cayenne's internal uses are as a stimulant, circulatory tonic, anti-spasmodic and diaphoretic; externally, it is a rubifacient (it produces burning warmth when rubbed on the skin), circulatory stimulant and antispasmodic.

*Chamomilla recutita and Anthema nobilis*

# Chamomile

Chamomile and peppermint are the only two herbs in this book which are widely sold as herbal teas. More and more herbs are being sold in teabags, but these two feature here not only because they are easily available but also because they are probably the most popular medicinal herbs in the world. Two varieties of chamomile are used in medicine. *Chamomilla recutita* – wild or German chamomile – is the species most often used in teabags. The picture is of *Anthemis nobilis* or double chamomile, varieties of which are used for lawns.

Chamomile flowers are calming and soothing and especially beneficial to the nerves and digestion. In medical terms they are anodyne, antiseptic, anti-inflammatory, antispasmodic and anti-allergic. They make an excellent regular drinking tea for people with a nervous disposition, or for anyone under stress.

Chamomile is the most suitable herb for infants and is used for colic, vomiting, loss of appetite, restlessness, nightmares, teething troubles and itchy skin rashes. A teaspoon or two of ordinary strength chamomile tea, three times a day, is all that

## 'BEHIND THE EARS' WASH

*a handful of chamomile flowers*
*600 ml/1 pint /2½ cups cider vinegar*

*Add the chamomile to the vinegar. Steep for 2 weeks, strain, bottle and label.*

*Grandmother's injunction to 'wash behind your ears!' applies to other intimate parts of the body as well. Use 1 teaspoon to 250 ml/8 fl oz/1 cup of water as a regular wash for the genitals, to restore skin pH and discourage fungal infections such as thrush. Use 2 teaspoons to 250 ml/8 fl oz/1 cup of water as a douche, or a wash, for vaginal or penile thrush or other itchy conditions in the area.*
*To prepare lint wipes for travelling, use 3 teaspoons of herb to 250 ml/8 fl oz/1 cup of water. Cut pieces of lint to fit neatly into an airtight tin and sprinkle enough of the mixture on to each piece to just dampen it.*

## MEDICINAL CHAMOMILE TEA

*For the best effect use 2 teabags, or 2 teaspoons of the loose herb, to a cup of boiling water. Brew the herb in a covered container or much of its virtue will be lost in the steam. A small teapot is ideal; a saucer on top of a cup makes an acceptable alternative.*
*Add honey if wished – heather and linden blossom complement the flavour well and add to the medicinal benefits. Keep the teabags and when they have cooled a little use them as a compress over the affected part.*
*Remember that in longstanding conditions, it will be necessary to continue the tea for some weeks or months to benefit from its cumulative effect.*
*People who dislike the taste of strong chamomile tea can take it weak or blend it with an Indian or fruit tea.*

is usually needed. This may be given directly or added to the baby's drinks. Another way is to add a cup or two of chamomile tea to the evening bath.

Chamomile is the best single herb for headaches, used as a tea and a compress. It is also useful for indigestion and stomach pains of any kind, dispelling tension from the whole digestive tract. Use the hot tea as an inhalant to relieve hayfever and other allergic conditions of the eyes, nose and lungs.

Use a strong tea (cold) as a compress or lotion for insect bites, stings, sore eyes and itchy skin conditions. It will also keep the hair fair, if regularly used as a rinse after washing.

Infused oil of chamomile is very relaxing. Try using it as an all-over body massage or in the bath. For eczema or for dry, irritable skin, oil the body with it after bathing. For insomnia, try a long soak in a chamomile bath followed by a cup of the tea about an hour before bed.

*'There is a remarkable property about the Camomile which some still believe in implicitly – that it is the plant's physician. Nothing is thought to keep a garden so healthy as plenty of Camomile about; it will even revive drooping and sickly plants if placed near them.'*

Frances A. Bardswell, *The Herb Garden* (1911)

## *Cinnamomum zeylanicum*
# Cinnamon

In the wild, cinnamon trees grow up to 18 m/60 ft high, but in cultivation they are cut off close to the ground so that a fresh crop of shoots is always available. The shoots are harvested every two years, and the tree eventually becomes a dense 2 m/ 7 ft bush. Young shoots are cut and the bark removed in two long strips. The outer bark is peeled away and the inner bark left to dry. As it dries, it curls into 'quills' which are folded into each other to make 'sticks', for transport.

The best cinnamon comes from Sri Lanka. A related tree, cassia (*Cinnamon cassia*), grows in China and is used in Chinese cooking and medicine. Cassia has the same properties as cinnamon, but a rougher, slightly bitter taste. Cinnamon essential oil is distilled from waste or broken bark. An oil is also extracted from the leaves.

Cinnamon is warming and drying and is an excellent remedy for colds and poor circulation. It is gentler than ginger, but has a more sustained action. The two herbs are often used together, and indeed the combination makes for very pleasant warming decoctions and wines. In general, it is best to make decoctions and wines with the whole quills and roots rather than with the powders, which

### CINNAMON TOAST

*50 g/2 oz/4 tablespoons light brown granulated sugar*
*1½ teaspoons ground cinnamon*
*small pinch of ground nutmeg (optional)*
*40 g/1½ oz/3 tablespoons butter*

*Mash the spices and sugar into the butter. Spread on wholemeal (whole wheat) bread, sliced very thinly. Put under a very hot grill until the sugar caramelizes.*

### CINNAMON AND GINGER DECOCTION

*This is excellent for warding off colds. It can also be used as a mouthwash for infected gums and unpleasant breath.*

*1½ cinnamon sticks (about 19 cm/7½ inches in all), broken up*
*about 2.5 cm/1 inch ginger root, sliced thinly*
*350 ml/12 fl oz/1½ cups water*
*1 teaspoon honey (optional)*

*Simmer the spices in the water in a tightly covered pan for 10 minutes. Strain and drink hot. Add honey if liked.*

### PARFAIT AMOUR

*The 'warming up' effect of cinnamon is used to good effect in this traditional French aphrodisiac liqueur.*

*15 cm/6 inches cinnamon stick*
*1 tablespoon fresh or dried thyme*
*¼ vanilla pod (bean)*
*1 teaspoon coriander seed*
*½ teaspoon mace, powdered or crushed*
*peel of 1 small lemon*
*600 ml/1 pint/2¼ cups vodka, or your favourite spirit*
*225 g/8 oz good honey (acacia, heather and 'mountain' honeys are best)*
*300 ml/½ pint/1¼ cups water*

*Crush the dry ingredients together as finely as possible, macerate in the spirits for 15 days and filter. Dissolve the honey in the water over gentle heat. Allow to cool and mix with the spiced spirits. Bottle and label. Dose: 50 ml/2 fl oz before bed.*

tend to make the drink muddy. Daily use of cinnamon drinks will help to clear up problems with cold hands and feet.

Chewing a stick of cinnamon is the simplest and quickest treatment for nose colds. An old cold cure was a glass of hot milk with 2 heaped teaspoons of ground cinnamon, a spoonful of honey and a good slug of brandy, taken at bedtime.

Cinnamon promotes digestion, clears wind and settles nausea. It has long been a favourite flavouring for cakes, biscuits (cookies) and apple pies. Apples stewed with a little cinnamon and served with low-fat live yogurt make an ideal healthy dessert, providing plenty of goodness and helping the digestive processes along. Cinnamon may also be used as a flavouring in chicken and pork dishes. One teaspoon of cinnamon powder stirred into a small glass of warm milk is a good remedy for diarrhoea and stomach upsets in children.

Cinnamon is used in the traditional Ayurvedic medicine of India to create freshness and to strengthen and energize the tissues. A pinch is often added to warm and stimulate the absorption of other remedies.

*Citrus limonum*

# Lemon

Oranges and lemons were once rare and precious fruits. To grow them in the cold northern climate, grand mansions built orangeries. In the southern states of the USA, around the Mediterranean and in other countries where the lemon grows freely, it has long been employed as a remedy for a whole range of ailments. All of it is used: the juice, the oil, the zest, the peel and the pips – a remedy kit that comes in one neat, easily transportable package.

Lemon juice is cooling and refreshing, with a clear, sharp taste that cleanses and tones the system. Everyone knows about taking lemon and honey for colds, an 'old wives remedy' so effective that it is sold in every chemist in the form of proprietary remedies. In any fever, lemon acts as a cooling diuretic, lowering temperature and helping the body eliminate toxins. The juice of 1 lemon diluted in 600 ml/1 pint/2½ cups of water, with honey to taste, may be

### LIVER CLEANSING TONIC

*freshly squeezed juice of ½ lemon*
*freshly squeezed juice of ½ grapefruit*
*2 tablespoons virgin olive oil.*

*Mix together and drink every morning for 5 days. This can be taken to dissolve gallstones under professional guidance.*

### THREADWORM REMEDY

*1 lemon*
*300 ml/½ pint/1¼ cups water*
*2 teaspoons honey*

*Crush the peel, pulp and pips of the lemon, cover with water and steep for 2 hours. Strain through a sieve (strainer), pressing the lemon to extract all the liquid. Discard the pulp. Add the honey and drink before bed. A decoction of the whole fruit is also used.*

### LEMON SKIN BALM

*This is a healing and nutritive lotion which moisturizes and softens chapped and sensitive skin. This simple recipe cannot be improved upon. Any vegetable oil can be used, but if you make it regularly it is worth buying the best quality oil you can afford. Sweet almond oil, wheatgerm oil or peach kernel oil all enrich the skin.*

*4 teaspoons lemon juice*
*8 teaspoons vegetable oil*
*1½–2 teaspoons clear honey*

*Mix the ingredients together thoroughly by putting them into a screwtop jar and shaking well.*
*A perfect body lotion can be made by adding an equal amount of water (1–1½ teaspoons). Shake continually while applying.*
*Both of these lotions are unperfumed, apart from the natural fragrance of the ingredients. One drop of essential oil may be added if extra fragrance is wanted.*

drunk freely. A cold compress made from the juice of 1 lemon to 1.2 litres/2 pints/5 cups of cold water will also reduce temperature and cool any swelling or surface heat. A lemon blanket bath and clean sheets make bed rest more bearable and are wonderfully refreshing.

Although lemon juice is acid to the taste and on the skin, within the body it is both an alkalizing agent and gastric antacid. It neutralizes excess acidity in the body and helps to remedy sluggishness of the liver and bowel.

Taking lemon juice every morning is a good way of maintaining health and warding off infections. It balances the nervous system, helping to reduce high blood pressure, protect blood vessels and maintain tissue vitality, and is also useful for alleviating rheumatism and gout. It contains a number of minerals and vitamins, including potassium, vitamins A, B and C and bioflavonoids.

On the skin, lemon juice is antiseptic for insect bites and a healing astringent for chapped skin and broken capillaries. Lemon oil is contained in pockets in the peel. The best way to obtain it is to squeeze the peel and rub it on the affected area. It is antiseptic, bactericidal and anti-fungal, and is useful for warts and ringworm.

*Cucumis sativus*

# Cucumber

Cucumber is cooling to the body, whether taken internally or externally. It is soothing, healing, demulcent and slightly diuretic.

Cucumber is an annual plant with large, irregularly toothed leaves. It climbs by means of tendrils. It is thought to have originated in southern Asia but the evidence is inconclusive, though it is known to have been cultivated for 3000 years and is mentioned in Egyptian writing in connection with the skin. The juice and preparations are unsurpassed for skin care and are used extensively in the cosmetic industry and perfumery. The smell is clear and sharp.

John Gerard, writing in 1597, recommends eating a potage made with cucumber and oatmeal three times a day: 'taken in this manner without intermission, doth perfectly cure all manner of sauce flegme and copper faces, red and shining fierie noses (as red as red Roses) with pimples, pumples, rubies, and such like precious faces. Provided always that during the time of

## CUCUMBER LOTION

*Rub the juice of 1 cucumber directly on to the skin. The juice can be preserved with an equal amount of vodka, in which case it should be used diluted in the same way as the following decoction.*

## CUCUMBER DECOCTION

*1 cucumber, chopped and crushed
600 ml/1 pint/2½ cups water*

*Macerate, then simmer for 10 minutes. Strain and use immediately, or preserve by slowly reducing to 150 ml/¼ pint/⅝ cup and adding 150 ml/¼ pint/⅝ cup vodka. This will keep indefinitely.
Use diluted 1 : 6 with water as a wash or compress; diluted 1 : 25 with water as a compress and eye bath.*

curing you do wash . . . the face with the following . . . [then comes a recipe of a cucumber lotion]. This doth not onely helpe fierie faces, but also taketh away lentils, spots, morphew, sunburne, and all other deformities of the face.'

The body should be a warm 37°C/98.4°F, and warmer at the core than at the extremities. If it is too hot and congested, or if a fever will not break, the body needs cooling. If it is too cold and stiff, gentle heat will get the blood circulating. If the body is warm and working well, do nothing! It is that simple; those are the three basic therapeutic actions. Cayenne is the herbal 'Sun' (see page 61) while cucumber is assigned to the 'Moon'. This recognizes cucumber's classic property to cool and heal 'Sun' damage (heat) or burns. With any burn (even sunburn) the first action is to cool the skin. If it is still 'burning', damage is still occurring. Apply cold running water, a slice of cucumber or a compress or ice pack until the pain stops. It may take several minutes to remove the heat from all the surrounding tissues. Then apply healing lotions or cooling balms.

Use cucumber lotion as a wash for fevers, congested headaches, hot tired eyes, hot throbbing feet and so on. The conditions that will benefit from cucumber become obvious once the actions of the plant are understood.

## CUCUMBER CURRY COMPLEMENTS

*With hot and cold in mind, here are two cucumber recipes. Both accompany very hot, spicy food.*

### Cold Complement

*½ cucumber, diced into 1 cm/½ inch cubes
1 teaspoon chopped fresh mint
100 g/4 oz live natural yogurt*

*Mix all the ingredients together. Serve chilled.*

### Warm Complement

*½ cucumber, diced into 1 cm/½ inch cubes
6 cloves of garlic, crushed and chopped finely
1 teaspoon salt
pinch of cayenne pepper (optional)*

*Mix the cucumber and garlic with the salt, cover and leave to stand for 2 hours. Serve at room temperature.*

## *Daucus carota*

# Carrot

Carrots are nourishing, easily digested and indeed soothing to the whole digestive system. They are a rich source of beta-carotene (the natural form of vitamin A), which has been shown to help protect the body against cancer and cholesterol and to strengthen night vision. They also provide vitamins B and C and iron, calcium, potassium, sugars and dietary fibre. The sugar gives carrots a sweet taste, which makes them a popular ingredient of soups, stews, cakes, salads and preserves. It is common knowledge that pure, refined sugar is bad for the teeth and excessive consumption can lead to reactive hypoglycaemia and, sometimes, to diabetes. The sugar in carrots, however, is in its unrefined, natural state, bound up with the fibre. It is only released into the system slowly, making carrots a much better source

## CARROT SALVE

*This very quick method of making a salve can be used for all vegetables, herbs and spices. Traditionally, oil, lard or animal fats were used. This is cooling, soothing and nutritive for chapped and dry skin.*

*2 carrots*
*oil to cover*
*beeswax*

*Grate the carrots, cover with oil and fry gently until the carrots are soft. The oil will turn orange. The oil can be strained and used as it is or you can turn up the heat and quickly fry until the carrots are dry and crisp, then strain. The oil is made into a salve by melting together 1 part beeswax to 5 parts oil.*

## CARROT PUDDING

*The sweetness in carrots is useful for overcoming sugar cravings. There are many recipes for carrot cake; this carrot pudding is an alternative.*

*350 g/12 oz/1½ cups carrots, cooked and mashed*
*100 g/4 oz/¾ cup raisins*
*100 g/4 oz/¾ cup currants*
*50 g/2 oz/½ cup plain (all-purpose) flour*
*175 g/6 oz/3 cups fresh breadcrumbs*
*100 g/4 oz/¾ cup suet or vegetable suet*
*½ teaspoon baking powder*
*75 g/3 oz/⅓ cup sugar or honey*
*1 teaspoon grated orange rind*
*grated nutmeg*
*pinch of salt*
*3 eggs, beaten*
*a little milk or water*

*Mix the carrots with the dry ingredients. Add the beaten eggs and a little milk or water to bring to a soft dropping consistency. Put the mixture in a greased basin, cover with greased greaseproof paper (baking parchment) and steam for 2½ hours.*

of sustained energy than sweets. A good way to break a sugar addiction is to carry a few carrots around in your pocket and nibble them whenever you feel the need. Because of their fibre content, chewing carrots is also good for the teeth. Eating raw carrots is an old-fashioned treatment for worms in children.

Carrots mashed, juiced or made into soup are an excellent food for convalescents, for the seriously ill and for children and old people with digestive upsets. Their soothing quality is a great help for people with hiatus hernia, gastritis, acidity and stomach ulcers, especially when taken before meals, and they will also soothe a raw, stubborn cough. They are good for the liver and kidneys and help the body to rid itself of toxins. A carrot fast – that is, eating nothing but carrots for a day or two – will clear out the system most efficiently, but the best way to take advantage of the great benefits of carrots is to eat them regularly as part of a balanced diet. Use mashed carrots as a poultice for painful swellings and for mastitis.

Vegetables should, if possible, be organic, especially those used for juice. Organic vegetables in general are much richer in nutrients than non-organic and they are, of course, free from the residue of pesticides. Organic carrots are widely available these days and the prices are falling as the demand grows.

*Elettaria cardamomum*

# Cardamom

Cardamom is a member of the ginger family but the seeds are the part used, rather than the root, as in ginger. It is a native of southern India and is cultivated there and in Central America. The whole seed pod is picked and dried very carefully in order to avoid it splitting open. In this way the full aromatic qualities of the seeds are preserved until needed. To use, split the pods open and crush the seeds to release their flavour.

The herbalist Peter Holmes, author of *The Energetics of Western Herbs* (Snow Lotus Inc., Boulder, USA, 1989) describes cardamom as having 'warm, pungent and sweet energies that qualify its restoring and stimulating action . . . [it] nourishes the stomach, intestines, nerves and brain'. The 'energy' of a herb describes its basic qualities. Cardamom is sweeter than ginger and therefore more nourishing (the sweetness is not due to sugar). It is a seed and therefore lighter than ginger, with a gentle warming action to the brain.

Learning to appreciate spices and herbs in this way helps you to use them more effectively. Start with the taste. Make a cup of cardamom tea and see if you agree with Peter's conclusions. Then make a cup of your favourite herbal tea and drink it slowly, trying to identify all the different flavours in it as you do so. How do they relate to what you know about its actions and uses?

## MIND MEDICINE

*This is a tasty, aromatic medicine for the brain. The herbs act together to calm anxiety, to promote mental alertness and clarity, to strengthen memory and to lift depression.*

*25 g/1 oz each of rosemary, cardamoms and fennel seeds*
*150 ml/¼ pint/⅝ cup vodka*
*150 ml/¼ pint/⅝ cup water*

*Crush the herbs, put them in a jar and cover with the liquids. Stand for 2 weeks, shaking occasionally. Strain, bottle and label. Take 2 or 3 teaspoons in a little water daily when needed.*

## TRADITIONAL CARDAMOM JUNKET

*Junkets must not be disturbed before serving or they will separate out. They are a traditional British food for children and convalescents, being nourishing and easily digestible. Common rennet is extracted from calves' stomachs and is thus not suitable for vegetarians. Vegetable rennet is available, but harder to come by.*

*8 large cardamom pods, crushed*
*475 ml/16 fl oz/2 cups milk*
*1 teaspoon clear honey*
*2 teaspoons essence of rennet*
*ground cinnamon*

*Simmer the cardamoms in the milk over very gentle heat for 5 minutes. Strain into a serving bowl, stir in the honey and allow to cool to blood heat (37°C/98.4°F). Stir in the rennet essence and put into a warm place until set, about 12 hours. Sprinkle ground cinnamon on top and serve.*

Cardamom is especially useful for depression and listlessness associated with chronic exhaustion and illness, sharpening the mind and lifting the spirits. It moves trapped intestinal wind and relieves colicky pains, and its mildness makes it more suitable for stomach troubles such as gastritis and vomiting than the hotter spices, which can sometimes upset an acid stomach. It is also chewed for sinusitis and to sweeten the breath. Added to foods and drinks made from milk, or milk products, it diminishes their tendency to promote catarrh. In many parts of the world it is added to tea and coffee to balance the over-stimulating effect of caffeine.

A small airtight jar of the following pot-pourri is excellent to keep on the desk while working – one sniff will clear the brain. Grind together 1 tablespoon each of rosemary and cardamom, 2 teaspoons cloves, 15 cm/6 inches cinnamon, the zest of 1 lemon, 2 teaspoons sea salt with enough brandy to make a damp paste.

# *Eugenia aromatica, syn. E. caryophyllus*
# Cloves

In ancient Chinese medical writing, cloves are one of the earliest medicinal spices mentioned. They are the dried flower buds of a tall evergreen tree of the *Myrtaceae* family. Clove oil is distilled from the buds, leaves and stalks.

In the 15th century the Portuguese discovered cloves growing in the Moluccas, a group of islands in Indonesia. They were one of the most expensive and precious spices, esteemed almost as a panacea. The Dutch gained control of the islands in the 17th century and had the monopoly of supply until planting material was smuggled out in the 18th century. Crops were then established in Zanzibar and Madagascar by the French.

## FIONA'S RUB

*This is for pulmonary infections. It also makes a good analgesic rub for backaches and headaches.*

*25 g/1 oz ground cloves*
*50 g/2 oz ginger root, grated*
*100 g/4 oz dried thyme*
*50 g/2 oz dried sage*
*50 g/2 oz dried rosemary*
*4 teaspoons cayenne pepper*
*600 ml/1 pint/2½ cups vegetable oil*

*Infuse together following the method on page 31. The oil can also be turned into a chest plaister.*

## FOUR THIEVES VINEGAR

*There is a popular tale that during the great plague in France, four thieves invented a herbal disinfectant vinegar to ward off infection so that they could rob the dead without fear. The vinegar worked and they grew rich. Eventually they were caught and plea-bargained with their recipe for a merciful death. There are several versions of the recipe – here is one.*

*1 teaspoon each ground clove, nutmeg and cinnamon*
*2 teaspoons each dried rosemary, peppermint and sage*
*2 teaspoons crushed garlic*
*1 litre/1¾ pints/4 cups cider vinegar*

*Put all the ingredients in a tightly covered glass vessel and stand in strong sunlight for 15 days. Strain and bottle. This can be used as a general disinfectant around the house.*

## CHILDBIRTH

*Drinking raspberry leaf tea in the last 3 months of pregnancy improves the tone of the womb. Cloves are a stimulating uterine tonic, preparing the womb for birth. During the last month of pregnancy start including cloves in the diet, in soup, apple pies and tea. At the onset of labour make a strong tea (5–6 cloves to a cup of water) and drink it freely throughout labour.*

Cloves, and clove oil, are most commonly used for relieving toothache, especially pain from infection and nerve exposure. A small wad of cotton wool is soaked in oil and held against the tooth, the anaesthetic quality bringing instant relief. In view of their well-established reputation for this, it is strange that cloves are not more widely used on other parts of the body where they would be equally effective – for example, infused oil of cloves makes an excellent analgesic rub for backaches and headaches.

Cloves are a very powerful antiseptic, germicide and disinfectant, killing bacteria, viruses, fungal infections and scabies. Just one clove will preserve beef for 24 hours. There is a story told that after the Dutch destroyed the clove trees on the island of Ternate in the early 17th century, it was swept by previously unknown epidemics.

Add 3 cloves to any infused tea or syrup to make a medicine for bronchial infections. Teas with cloves can also be used as a mouthwash for oral hygiene and toothache. Use externally as a wash, lotion or compress for infected wounds.

The warmth of cloves calms the stomach and aids digestion. Mrs Maud Grieves, author of the classic *A Modern Herbal* (1931), says: 'Give in a powder or infusion for nausea, flatulence, languid indigestion and dyspepsia.'

The deep, distinctive smell of cloves reassures the body and raises the spirits. For a mildly stimulating morning drink, add 1–2 cloves to any tea.

Make an infused massage oil for helping women in childbirth from 1 part cloves and 3 parts lavender flowers. Massage into the lower back using smooth, circular strokes.

*Ficus carica*

# Figs

Originally from western Asia and now in cultivation all over the world, figs were a major item of commerce in ancient times. In his *Natural History* (AD77), the Roman writer Pliny names no fewer than 29 different varieties. The athletes of Sparta were said to have lived on figs, regarding them as a great aid to strength and swiftness.

Figs are nutritious and easily digestible, but they are probably best-known for their gentle laxative action, which is particularly suitable for treating constipation in children. This laxative property is due to a combination of fruit sugars and fibre. Add a few fresh or dried figs to breakfast dishes – for example, chopped figs make a tasty addition to wholegrain cereals. Syrup of figs is still a popular standby and is often used as a base for stronger laxatives, such as senna. The best long-term treatment for constipation is, of course, eating more dietary fibre such as is found in fruit, green vegetables and wholegrain cereals.

Figs are soothing to the lungs and were much used for treating chronic lung diseases, either in cakes or syrups.

## COUGH REMEDY FROM A 17TH-CENTURY STILL-ROOM BOOK

*'Take a handful of Hysop; of Figs, Raisins, Dates of each an ounce, French Barley one ounce, boyl therein three pintes of fair water to a quart, strain it and clarifie with two Whites of Eggs, then put in two pounds of fine Sugar and boyl it to a syrup.'*

From *The Queen's Closet Opened* (1655) by 'W.M.', cook to Queen Henrietta Maria of England.

*This can easily be adapted, using the basic syrup-making method on page 40. If you cannot find hyssop, use thyme instead. Clarifying is not absolutely necessary, but it does make for a more attractive result – obviously important when making medicines for a queen.*

## APERIENT FIG CAKES

*100 g/4 oz/⅔ cup dried figs*
*100 g/4 oz/⅔ cup raisins*
*1 teaspoon ground ginger or ½ teaspoon ground nutmeg*

*Pound the ingredients together well in a pestle and mortar (or use a food processor). Roll into a sausage 2.5 cm/1 inch thick and cut into 1 cm/½ inch slices. Store in an airtight tin or jar.*
*Dose: 1 or more slices a day, or when needed.*

## SYRUP OF FIGS

*8 dried figs*
*250 ml/8 fl oz/1 cup water*
*225 g/8 oz/1 cup molasses or dark brown sugar*
*juice of ½ lemon*
*1 teaspoon ground ginger*

*Slice the figs thinly and simmer them in the water until soft, about 20 minutes. Pour the liquid off and set the figs aside. Make the liquid back up to the original amount with fresh water, add the molasses or sugar and heat gently, stirring all the time, until the sugar is dissolved. Add the lemon juice, ginger and figs and blend in a blender or food processor. Pour into a clean, preferably sterilized jar, label and store in a cool place. It will keep well. Dose: For a child, 1–2 dessertspoons daily; for an adult, 3–4 dessertspoons daily.*

Figs have been used to make applications for treating skin diseases for thousands of years. Some 2700 years ago the prophet Isaiah advised King Hezekiah to apply dried mashed figs to his boils. Whole fresh figs roasted and split in half can also be used as a handy poultice for boils and gumboils. The milky-white juice that exudes from the stalks of fig leaves when freshly cut makes a good wart cure, but care should be taken to apply it only to the wart as it can blister ordinary skin. Ointments and creams made from fresh fig leaves are healing and cooling for itchy skin problems and for piles.

## *Foeniculum vulgare*

# Fennel

In William Langland's *The Vision of William Concerning Piers Plowman* (1377), the Alewife says, 'I have pepper and paeony seed and a pound of garlick, and a farthingworth of fennel seed, for fasting days.' Chewing fennel seeds calms the stomach and makes it easier to fast. The Greeks use it to help lose weight – but remember that there is no substitute for a well-balanced diet and adequate exercise when it comes to long-term weight control. Fennel's carminative action makes it useful for any kind of indigestion or wind problems. As a sauce it balances the flavour of fish and mushrooms and aids their digestion, while in India, fennel seeds and aniseeds are mixed together and chewed after meals. A few teaspoons of fennel seed tea will wind a baby and relieve colic more efficiently than any commercial gripe water. Nursing mothers should take fennel tea every day, not only to cure their baby's wind problems but also to ensure a good supply of milk.

Like parsley, to which it is related, fennel is diuretic and can be used for combating water retention and relieving premenstrual breast-swelling. It is also useful to drink and eat as part of a regime for arthritis.

Drinking fennel tea regularly is said to strengthen the eyesight and it makes an effective wash or compress for sore and inflamed eyes.

In Indian medicine, fennel is said to be perfectly balanced – neither too heating nor too cooling. It is excellent for people who cannot tolerate very hot condiments and its balancing action extends to the nervous system; it calms the nerves, uplifts the spirits and promotes mental clarity. The 12th-century visionary and herbalist Hildegard von Bingen said, 'Fennel forces [a person] back into the right balance of joyfulness.' The smell has the quickest effect. This can be released by heating the seeds and inhaling the smoke or by making an infused oil for massage. **CAUTION:** DO NOT TAKE LARGE AMOUNTS OF FENNEL SEEDS WHEN PREGNANT. The amounts used in cooking are safe.

*Above the lowly plants it towers,*
*The fennel, with its yellow flowers,*
*And in an earlier age than ours*
*Was gifted with the wondrous powers,*
*Lost vision to restore.*
*It gave new strength, and fearless mood;*
*And gladiators, fierce and rude,*
*Mingled it in their daily food;*
*And he who battled and subdued,*
*A wreath of fennel wore.*

From 'The Goblet of Life' by Henry Wadsworth Longfellow (1846)

---

### 'SMOKING' FENNEL

*'Smoking' herbs, or inhaling the smoke of burning herbs, relaxes the chest muscles. Fumigation, or immersing the whole body in smoke, gives all-over relaxation. The Lacnunga, a 10th-century Anglo-Saxon medical text, recommends, 'Take fennel and hassuck [dried grass or rushes] and cotton and burn all together on the side which the wind is.' It recommends the practitioner to 'reek' patients with steam. This brings to mind the Native American practice of sweat lodges. Smoke is also used in purification rituals.*

### SMOKE INHALANT

*2 teaspoons fennel seeds, crushed*
*1 teaspoon aniseed, crushed*
*1 pinch grated nutmeg*

*To use, put a small amount on the hotplate of a cooker. Inhale the smoke. Special charcoal blocks are made on which powdered herbs can be burnt. If you have these, powder the herbs very finely, using a pestle and mortar or a clean coffee grinder. The same mixture can be used as a steam inhalation.*

*Hordeum distichon and H. vulgare*

# Barley

Barley is nourishing and demulcent. At one time it was the dominant grain crop in Europe but was superseded by wheat, which originated in the Middle East. Roman gladiators and Greek shepherds ate cakes made with barley and goat's milk for strength and vigour, and cakes made with barley and other grains were eaten at festivals.

Many societies still eat a wide range of cereals in their bread. It would be much healthier for us, and indeed for our planet too, to grow and eat a wider range of cereals rather than concentrating so heavily on the high-gluten wheat that is used in large-scale bread-making. These days, barley is mostly used for making malt, malt vinegar, beer and spirits and for thickening soups and stews. Malt, which is made from sprouted barley grains, was once a favourite 'strengthening medicine' for children.

Whole or pot barley contains vitamins B and E, calcium, potassium, protein and starch. It helps to lower blood cholesterol levels. Pearl barley has had much of the goodness removed

### BARLEY WATER

*1 part pearl barley, washed*
*9 parts water*
*lemon juice*

*Simmer the barley and water together for 20 minutes, strain and add lemon juice to taste. Drink freely.*
*Other cooling juices can be used instead of the lemon juice. Children are especially fond of barley water made with blackcurrant juice. Use pure juices rather than fruit 'drinks' with sugar added.*
*The water can be replaced by herbal teas: thyme tea for coughs and stomach infections, sage tea for sore throats, parsley or fennel tea for cystitis.*
*Barley water will keep in a cool place for 3–4 days, or longer if extra lemon juice is added.*

from it along with the husk, but it still has a useful place in food and medicine.

The cooling action of barley is used in drinks for fevers. Its soothing and healing actions are used, again in drinks, for stomach acidity, digestive upsets, irritable bowels, dry coughs, cystitis and irritable bladders. Barley water is the best preparation for all these conditions. Home-made barley water is a much better medicine than commercial products and is well worth the little extra effort needed to prepare it.

Strong barley water soothes sore throats and makes an excellent wash for raw, itchy rashes. Barley poultices are used to draw the poison from boils, abcesses, stings and bites and also to clear up weeping eczema. Barley may be added to any herbal medicine when a little extra soothing is needed.

Grains are used in other foods, such as soups, as well as in breads. We could and should eat more. Soups containing barley are simple to prepare, but even easier is a basic winter soup mix that is sometimes sold containing lentils, split peas, butter beans and barley. This is soaked overnight and then boiled with seasoning to provide a base of vegetable protein to which fresh seasonal vegetables can be added. Such thick soups are a cheap and effective form of nourishment.

### BARLEY POULTICES

*These are based on flaked barley or barley flour. Use a clean coffee grinder to make flour from pearl or pot barley. Add sufficient boiling water to make a paste, wrap in a piece of clean cloth or a paper towel and apply hot or cold.*

*A simple poultice, applied hot, will ease stiff and painful joints and draw poisons from abscesses and infected cuts. Add herbs to the barley flour, in equal parts, for particular effects; chamomile for any deep pain and stomach aches, sage for aching joints, onion for boils, abscesses and infected cuts.*

*Adding honey to barley flour makes a paste suitable for weeping eczema and other itchy skin conditions.*

*According to Culpeper, 'barley flour, white salt, honey and vinegar mingled together taketh away the itch speedily and certainly'.*

*Juniperus communis*

# Juniper Berries

Juniper is a small tree which is usually found growing on poor soil in mountainous or hilly country. The refreshing, distinctive smell is very evocative of warm days in high country. The berries are used in cooking to balance the strong flavour of game and to give a unique taste to bean stews. They are also responsible for the distinctive flavour of gin. In medicine they are digestive, warming and antiseptic as well as diuretic. Two or three berries added to fennel or sage tea will increase their effectiveness in treating arthritis and rheumatism. Add 3–4 berries to a cup of barley decoction to make an effective treatment for cystitis. The cleansing properties of juniper were traditionally extended to cleaning a new home of the feelings left behind by the previous occupants. If you want to try this yourself, make a full-strength decoction, put it in a clean plant spray and use it to spray all the rooms and corners.

Juniper and corn silk are both used for their diuretic properties. They both increase the flow of urine, reducing water retention, flushing poisons and waste products from the body and washing out the urinary tract. They are, however, two very different herbs: juniper is a stimulating diuretic and therefore best used for short periods and in small doses, while corn silk is a soothing and restorative diuretic and is thus more suitable for long-term use, or for when the kidneys are weak or damaged. If in doubt, use corn silk (see page 79).

**CAUTION:** JUNIPER SHOULD NOT BE USED INTERNALLY IN PREGNANCY (the amounts used in cooking are safe).

## JUNIPER FOR THE SKIN

*Juniper tincture or reduced decoction diluted 1–3 teaspoons to 250 ml/8 fl oz/1 cup water makes an excellent lotion or compress for weeping eczema, acne, sores, atonic wounds and ulcers. It can also be used as a soak to loosen stuck dressings. Many people are tempted to use undiluted lotions in the belief that as they are stronger they will be more effective. This is not the case – the aim is for the herbal remedy to enhance rather than obliterate the skin's delicate microflora in order to help the healing properties of the body.*

*As with all lotions for the skin, start with the weakest dilution and try to find the minimum effective dilution for your particular skin type.*

## JUNIPER SOAKS

*Juniper is anti-rheumatic, which means that it promotes the excretion of uric acid and toxins. Baths, handbaths and footbaths of juniper sometimes bring about spectacular results in rheumatism and arthritis. Add 1 tablespoon of reduced juniper decoction to 4.5 litres/8 pints/5 quarts of water, or use fresh juniper berry tea diluted in 600 ml/1 pint/2½ cups of water. Soak for 15–20 minutes. Repeat daily.*

*A suitable tea to accompany the soaks would be:*
*1 part fennel seeds*
*4 parts dried sage*
*1 part juniper berries*

*Crush the seeds and blend well with the sage. Use 1 teaspoon per cup. Dose: 1–2 cups per day.*

## JUNIPER AND RASPBERRY WATER ICE

*Water ices and herb slushes are a very pleasant way of cooling the body when it is hot and restless. A favourite with children is chamomile slush (chamomile tea with honey and crushed ice). This recipe serves 2–3 people.*

*1 tsp juniper decoction or tincture*
*250 ml/8 fl oz/1 cup raspberry purée*
*1 egg white*

*Mix the juniper and raspberry, put in the freezer until partially frozen, then take out and beat into a slush. Beat the egg white until stiff and then fold it into the raspberry mixture. Put into separate glasses and freeze for 2 hours. Serve with a sprig of fresh mint and small sweet biscuits.*

## *Mentha piperita*

# Peppermint

Peppermint is warming, antispasmodic, carminative, stimulant, antiseptic and decongestant. It is the mint most commonly used in herbal medicine, although all the mints can be used. Apple mint, lemon mint, curled mint and spearmint all have their own character, yet share basic properties.

Peppermint has been used since ancient times. In his *Natural History*, written in AD77 and reproduced here from a translation of 1601, Pliny says: 'As touching garden Mint, as the very smell of it alone recovereth and refresheth the spirits; so the tast stirreth up the appetite to meat, which is the cause, that it is so ordinarie in our sharpe sauces wherein we use to dip our meats . . . It is singular to drie up the humours that mollifie the grisly wind pipe and the other instruments of the breath and voice, and when they are drie, knitteth and strengthens them. Taken in water and honied wine, it clenseth the corrupt and putrefied flegmaticke humours which bee offensive to the

### COLDS AND FLU

*The traditional cold and flu tea is made of equal parts of peppermint, yarrow and elderflower. This tea is the magic cure-all, as it addresses all the elements present at the beginning of a cold. Taken as soon as the symptoms start, it will help the body re-establish balance quickly. Peppermint is the decongestant, yarrow is febrifuge, elderflower is a nose and throat tonic.*

*When you have a cold, remember all the methods of using herbs: teas, baths, rubs with infused oils, plaisters, cooling remedies, tonic drinks, inhalants and gargles. It is better to treat a symptom locally and effectively than to drench the body with unnecessary systemic medicines.*

*Pliny mentions the use of mint as being so common that 'all the meats from one end [of the country] to the other be seasoned with Mints'.*

throat and those parts. The juice of Mints is excellent for to scoure the pipes and clear the voice, being drunk a little before that a man is to straine himselfe either in the quier [choir], or upon the stage, or at the bar.'

Peppermint tea relaxes spasms in the digestive tract and is the best medicine for excess wind, hiccoughs and colicky pains. Peppermint settles the digestion very quickly when it has been upset by rushed meals. In the Middle East it is taken as a regular tea after meals.

Peppermint mixes well with other herbs, adding a depth of flavour sometimes missing from herb teas. For chronic griping pains due to weak digestion, try a regular tea of peppermint and marigold. For heavy colds with a blocked nose try peppermint and chamomile tea, inhaling the steam as you drink it. Some people find this mixture helpful for insomnia, especially when there is a lot of tension in the body, but strong mint teas keep others awake. Peppermint and sage tea, with a little honey, makes a good gargle for sore throats and for clearing mucus stuck in the back of the throat.

Massage with peppermint infused oil for general weakness, muscle weakness, fevers, bunions and itchy skin conditions.

### MINT SAUCE

*8 g/¹/₄ oz fresh mint*
*cider vinegar to cover*
*pinch each of cayenne, salt and sugar (optional)*

*Chop the mint and cover with vinegar. Add a pinch of cayenne, salt and sugar if liked.*

### APPLE MINT JELLY

*1 kg/2 lb tart green apples*
*8 g/¹/₄ oz mint*
*15 ml/1 tablespoon cider vinegar or juice of 1 lemon*
*pinch each of cayenne, salt and sugar (optional)*

*Chop the apples, skin, pips and all, and put in a saucepan. Add the mint and cider vinegar or lemon juice and enough water to cover, bring to the boil and simmer for 30 minutes until the fruit is a soft pulp. Strain through a jelly bag, allowing it to drip overnight. Return the liquid to the heat and reduce slowly to a syrupy consistency. This will set when cool.*

## *Petroselinum crispum*

# Parsley

Parsley has carminative, tonic, aperient and antiseptic diuretic action. It is useful for kidney, bladder and urinary tract infections. A strong decoction of the root is used for gravel, stone and congestion of the kidney, water retention and jaundice. Parsley tea proved very useful in the trenches during the First World War, where men often developed kidney complications following dysentery. Used as a poultice, it clears the skin of spots and eruptions.

These are general uses, but parsley is especially useful for women, hence its traditional reputation as a female 'corrective'. It helps women in a variety of ways, stimulating appetite, aiding digestion, speeding elimination, soothing the nerves by removing that overful, submerged, premenstrual feeling, bloating and PMT anxiety. The oestrogenic factors in the plant are water-balancing, stimulating to the uterus and relaxing to smooth muscles such as those of the heart and uterus; they relieve the build-up of internal stresses, headaches and cramps. Parsley brings on delayed menstrual flow and will help to normalize a slow, clotty flow. Taken daily, it will relieve unpleasant manifestations of the menopause by helping the body to maintain balance. It also provides necessary minerals including iron and calcium and vitamins A and C.

### SOUPE A LA BONNE FEMME

*This soup promotes good health in women.*

*40 g/1½ oz/3 tablespoons butter*
*40 g/1½ oz/6 tablespoons flour*
*1 teaspoon salt*
*1 medium onion, whole*
*600ml/1 pint/2½ cups cow's milk or soya milk*
*250 ml/8 fl oz/1 cup water*
*2 egg yolks, beaten*
*120 ml/4 fl oz/½ cup single (light) cream*
*100 g/4 oz fresh parsley, finely chopped*

*Melt the butter and add the flour, salt, onion, milk and water. Bring to the boil and simmer for 1 hour. Remove the onion. Add the beaten egg yolks and cream, if using. Cook gently, without boiling, until the soup thickens. Just before serving, add the parsley. Serve at once. Garlic croûtons make a strengthening addition.*

### JOY'S WISE WOMAN'S TONIC

*Good nutrition is particularly important for women, and especially so during the menopause when the body is readjusting to a new balance and afterwards to maintain health and strength. Calcium is found in parsley and cabbage, but for those needing an extra supplement try this tonic.*

*1 organic eggshell*
*juice of 1 lemon*
*15 g/½ oz parsley, fresh or dried*
*15 g/½ oz sage, fresh or dried*
*15 g/½ oz fennel seed*
*2 teaspoons honey (optional)*

*Scrub the eggshell, remove the membrane from inside and crush the shell. Cover with lemon juice and leave to stand until the eggshell dissolves into a white sediment (2–3 days). Make 75 ml/2½ fl oz/⅓ cup of decoction from the herbs (see page 18) and add this to the mixture. Strain, add honey to taste if liked, and bottle.*
*To use: Shake well and take 2–3 teaspoons a day.*

### WHOLE EGG AND CALCIUM STRENGTHENING TONIC

*2 organic eggs (from salmonella-free stock)*
*juice of 4 lemons*
*8 oz/225 g/1¼ cups brown sugar or honey*
*30 ml/2 tablespoons oil*
*600 ml/1 pint/2½ cups rum, wine or other spirit*

*Clean the eggs, put them in a bowl and pour the lemon juice over them. Leave to stand until the shells disappear (2–3 days). Beat the eggs, beat in the sugar or honey and strain through a piece of muslin (cheesecloth). Add the oil and alcohol. Store in the refrigerator.*
*To use: Take 25 ml/1 fl oz/1¾ tablespoons night and morning.*

Parsley is so important for women that Billy Potts, author of *Witches Heal* (Iowa City Women's Press, 1981), ends her section on it by reclaiming parsley for women as a companion plant, a vital supporter in the female pharmacopoeia.

**CAUTION:** DO NOT TAKE THE ROOT IN PREGNANCY. DO NOT TAKE THE SEEDS AT ALL.

## *Pimpinella anisum*

# Aniseed

Not to be confused with the star anise, which has a stronger taste and action, aniseed is the small seed (properly the fruit) of an annual plant belonging to the *Umbelliferae* family (the same family as coriander, parsley and fennel).

Aniseed has an excellent, warming flavour popular in confectionery and pastries. It is a valuable digestive, curing flatulence and helping the assimilation of food. Its action on the lungs is both calming and stimulating, a useful combination for asthma, bronchial spasm, coughs and wheeziness in general. Like fennel, aniseed is a spice with a built-in feel-good factor. It helps us to overcome the stresses of illness, so that more energy can be directed towards healing. Taken warm with honey, the tea is good for small children suffering from diarrhoea, colic, asthma or hiccups. If fennel is added it helps to ease bronchial catarrh. The fumes relax the chest and the seeds can be ground and added to a chest plaister. Chewing aniseed induces sleep.

Aniseed is probably best-known as a flavouring in drinks such as Pernod, anisette and ouzo. With water and ice these are wonderfully relaxing yet cooling drinks, ideal for a hot day by the Mediterranean sea. At high and prolonged doses it is a stupefacient and was one of the ingredients of absinthe, along with wormwood. This was the popular drug for the bohemian circles of the Left Bank in Paris in the last century.

### THE REVIVER

*This is powerful stuff for healing contusions and easing toothache. It is also good mixed with oil for a liniment. Try 1 teaspoon in water, with honey to taste, after falls and shocks.*

*Makes 280 ml/9 fl oz/1 cup plus 2 tablespoons*
*2 teaspoons ground clove*
*1 teaspoon ground cinnamon*
*1 teaspoon ground ginger*
*2 teaspoons aniseed, crushed*
*300ml/½ pint/1¼ cups vodka*

*Macerate all the ingredients together for 6 weeks, strain and bottle.*

### LIQUEUR OF ANISEED
*Makes 475 ml/16 fl oz/2 cups*

*2 tablespoons crushed aniseed*
*5 cm/2 inches cinnamon quill, crushed*
*1 nutmeg, crushed (optional)*
*2 tablespoons honey*
*200 ml/7 fl oz/⅞ cup brandy*
*300 ml/½ pint/1¼ cups water*

*Mix all the ingredients together and macerate for 6 weeks, shaking occasionally. Filter and bottle. Take 50 ml/2 fl oz/¼ cup after meals as a carminative digestive or before bed as an aphrodisiac.*

### ANISEED DIGESTIVE BISCUITS
*Makes about 60 biscuits*

*8 g/¼ oz aniseed*
*250 g/9 oz butter*
*225 g/8 oz caster sugar (keep 3 teaspoons separate to sprinkle on top)*
*3 drops vanilla flavouring (extract)*
*15 ml/1 tablespoon rum*
*15 ml/1 tablespoon milk or water*
*350 g/12 oz/3 cups plain (all-purpose) flour*
*beaten egg yolk or milk*

*Crush the aniseed, leaving a small amount uncrushed to use for decoration. Heat the butter in a pan until brown, then leave to cool. Beat in one-third of the sugar, then add the remainder with the vanilla flavouring (extract), rum, milk or water and crushed aniseed. Mix in the flour thoroughly, then turn out on to a board and knead well. Shape into long, thin rolls and cool in a refrigerator for 1 hour.*

*Cut into rounds about 30 cm/12 inches thick and put on to a greased baking sheet (cookie sheet), spaced well apart. Brush with beaten egg yolk or milk, and sprinkle with whole aniseed and caster sugar. Bake in a preheated oven at 180°C/350°F/Gas Mark 4 for 8–10 minutes until golden brown. Allow to cool for 2–3 minutes before removing from the rack.*

The digestive property of aniseed is shared with other aromatic spices and has been used since classical times. Romans would eat spicy cakes containing aniseed after a rich meal. This is thought to be the origin of the spicy wedding cake of today.

## *Rosmarinus officinalis*
# Rosemary

Rosemary is an evergreen, half-hardy shrub, flowering in late winter or early spring. It makes a classic bitter tonic, strengthening the digestion and improving liver function. Such herbs are the best for long-term improvement of digestive dysfunction. Take a small glass of rosemary wine as an aperitif about half an hour before meals so that the digestive system is primed and made ready for the work to come. Eating food in a hurry, and with the digestion unprepared, is the commonest cause of abdominal pain and spasm.

Rosemary is also a circulatory tonic, invaluble for all cases of poor circulation and aches and pains that come with the cold. Long-term use of rosemary tea will improve a whole range of symptoms in people with poor circulation. The infused oil is used for massage of cold joints and aching muscles. It also has a reputation for strengthening the heart and calming palpitations. The official German *Pharmacopoeia* contains a recipe for a rosemary massage oil to rub in over the region of the heart. Rosemary is a nerve tonic, too, and this combination of properties makes it a good herb for relieving the pains of neuralgia. Again, it is taken as a tea and used as a massage oil. Since it is a stimulant, it is best not to take rosemary just before bed.

Rosemary has a particular application to the head. It is combined with chamomile for headaches, with cardamom for depression and is used by itself for improving scalp condition, strengthening hair growth and preventing premature baldness. For a dry scalp, rub rosemary infused oil well in and leave for 30 minutes before washing out with a gentle shampoo. For weak hair with a greasy scalp, make rosemary vinegar and add 2 dessertspoons to the final rinsing water.

Bushes of rosemary are often grown in graveyards and mourners would carry a sprig to throw into the grave as a symbol of remembrance. This is more than just a symbol, for rosemary really does strengthen the memory by improving the blood flow to the head and stimulating the nervous system. The traditional and symbolic use of plants usually reflects their actual medical properties. Ancient wisdom should not be ignored as it is often verified by scientific research and updated for modern usage.

---

### A BREATH FRESHENER

*'The distilled water of Rosemary flowers being drunke at morning and evening first and last, taketh away the stench of the mouth and breathe, and maketh it very sweet, if there be added thereto, to steep or infuse for certaine dais, a few cloves, mace, cinnamon and a little aniseed.'*

John Gerard, *The Herball or Generall Historie of Plants*, 1597

*Distilled waters are hard to come by, so make a tincture of all these herbs and use 2 teaspoons in a glass of water as a mouthwash.*

---

### ROSEMARY TEA AS A 'SIMPLE'

*250 ml/8 fl oz/1 cup water
1 teaspoon chopped rosemary*

*Boil the water and pour it on to the rosemary. Leave to steep for a few minutes, then strain and serve. This is an ideal tea for taking with friends. There is nothing quite so good for lifting the spirits and cheering the heart as a cup of rosemary tea taken in good company.*

*'Let this rosmarinus, this flower of men, ensigns of your wisdom, love and loyalty be carried not only in your hands but in your heart and heads.'*

From a sermon by the Rev. Roger Hacket, 1607

*Salvia officinalis*

# Sage

Like a number of our common cooking herbs, sage originates from the Mediterranean, although the plant will withstand a few degrees of frost in colder climates once established. It has a strong taste and is generally used to flavour the richer meats such as pork, duck and goose. It aids in the digestion of fats. There are several varieties of sage, all of which share the same medicinal properties.

For centuries, sage has been highly regarded as a medicine, as shown by the traditional saying, 'Why should a man die whilst sage grows in his garden?' It is a general tonic, useful for weak and exhausted states and particularly good for the tiredness that typically follows a viral infection. It tones the central nervous system and lifts the spirits. Sage tea with honey is ideal for that end-of-the-day, worn-down-by-life feeling. It also helps concentration and is therefore a good tea for students.

Fresh sage leaves, eaten in sandwiches for breakfast, is an English country cure for low-grade fevers and flu symptoms. Sage tea, taken cold, is the best treatment for excessive sweating. Two or three cups a day, taken for three weeks, will usually do the trick.

Sage has a high resin content, which makes it antiseptic and slightly sticky, an ideal combination for treating sore throats and mouth and gum infections. It is the herbalists' favourite for gargles, mouthwashes and tooth powders. Strong sage tea is a simple and effective wash for infected and inflamed cuts. It is also a useful hair treatment: a cup or two of sage tea, added to the final rinsing water, will gradually darken the hair and keep the scalp healthy.

Sage is a very helpful herb for women. Taken internally and used as a compress, it soothes painful, lumpy breasts. It helps to regulate periods, can bring on delayed periods and dries up breast milk. Sage is especially useful at the change of life, helping to diminish hot flushes and lift depression.

**CAUTION:** DO NOT TAKE SAGE AS A MEDICINE WHEN PREGNANT OR BREASTFEEDING. The small amounts used in cooking present no problems.

*'Sage strengths the sinewes, fevers heat doth swage,*
*The palsy helps, and rids of muckle woe.*
*In Latin [Salvia] takes the name of safety*
*In English [Sage] is rather wise than crafty*
*Sith then the name betokens wise and saving*
*We count it nature's friend and worth the having.'*

Sir John Harington, *The Englishman's Doctor* (1607).
This poem is a memory aid, in verse, to help students learn.

---

## TRADITIONAL SAGE AND ONION SAUCE

*½ small onion, chopped finely*
*15 g/½ oz dried sage*
*120 ml/4 fl oz/½ cup water*
*1 teaspoon salt*
*1 teaspoon pepper*
*25 g/1 oz breadcrumbs*
*300 ml/½ pint/1¼ cup stock*

*Put the onion, sage and water in a small pan and simmer gently for 10 minutes. Add the salt, pepper and breadcrumbs and mix well. Add the stock slowly, stirring well. Simmer together for a few minutes and pour over the roast meat.*

## SAGE AND NUTMEG INFUSED OIL

*75 g/3 oz dried or 100 g/4 oz fresh sage, chopped*
*1 teaspoon ground nutmeg*
*300 ml/½ pint/1¼ cup sunflower oil*

*Make the ingredients into an infused oil (see page 31).*
*Use as a massage oil for twitchy, overexcited people and for numb and paralysed limbs.*

**CAUTION:** DO NOT USE IN PREGNANCY.

*Thymus vulgaris*

# Thyme

Thyme is a popular culinary and garden plant with a number of different varieties, all having much the same use in cooking and medicine. It likes a sunny spot and light soil and will thrive in most window-boxes. In the garden, it is best planted in paths – the more it is trodden on, the stronger it will smell. The fragrance is uplifting and energizing. In the Middle Ages, ladies would give thyme sprigs to their champions to help them maintain their courage in jousting tournaments.

Thyme is strongly antiseptic. (The essential oil of thyme has been shown to be 20 times stronger than phenol, the standard antiseptic.) It is also antispasmodic and expectorant. This combination of properties makes it an excellent medicine for all lung diseases. Syrup of thyme is a handy standby for all types of cough and wheeziness, in children and adults. Traditionally, thyme was regarded as a specific for spasmodic coughs – a tradition which has been since borne out by modern research. Use the infused oil as a chest massage to back up the internal use of the tea or syrup.

Thyme is also useful for intestinal and bladder infections. Using antiseptic herbs for non-serious infections is preferable to using antibiotics, which upset the balance of good bacteria in the digestive tract. Excessive use of antibiotics is responsible for a number of chronic complaints, including candida, which produces wind, bloating and low energy levels. You should, of course, consult your doctor about infections before treating yourself. If you need to take antibiotics eat plenty of live yogurt at the same time to maintain the balance of internal flora. Thyme tea is one of the best anti-candida remedies.

Thyme is anti-fungal, and the vinegar can be used to treat fungal infections on the skin. In Scotland, thyme tea is taken to prevent nightmares and ease headaches.

**CAUTION:** STRONG THYME TEAS ARE BEST AVOIDED IN PREGNANCY.

## ROBERT'S AROMATIC HERB JAR

*The name 'thyme' comes from a Greek word meaning 'fumigation', an allusion to the healing properties of its smoke. The smell of thyme lifts depression and calms anxiety. To make good use of this property, find a attractive pot with a lid and fill it with good-quality dried thyme and other uplifting herbs. Leave it in an easily accessible place. When you walk past it, lift the lid, dip your hand in and rub the herbs through your fingers. Run your fingers through your hair or over your clothes so that the smell lingers.*

## SUN-INFUSED THYME VINEGAR

*This is best made using fresh thyme. Crush the herb and loosely fill a large jar. Cover with wine or cider vinegar and stand outside for 40 days to catch any sunshine. Strain off the vinegar and discard the thyme. Fill the jar with fresh thyme, cover with the same vinegar and stand outside for another 40 days. This vinegar can be used as a general household disinfectant – and it comes with its own natural scent!*

## SABINE'S YUMMY COUGH SYRUP

*This is soothing, antiseptic, antibiotic and expectorant. It thins out the mucus and opens out the bronchi. Use for a deep, restless, chesty cough, tightness and sore throat.*

*15 g/½ oz dried thyme*
*8 g/¼ oz dried sage*
*8 g/¼ oz dried chamomile*
*2 teaspoons fennel seeds*
*1 teaspoon aniseed*
*20 cloves*
*2 garlic cloves*
*pinch of cayenne pepper or ground ginger*
*900 ml/1½ pints/3¾ cups water*
*450 g/1 lb honey*

*Use all the ingredients to make a syrup (see page 40).*

## Zea mays
# Corn Silk

Corn silk is the yellow or gingery 'hairs' (stigmas and styles) of whole sweetcorn. When fresh corn is on sale the silk is beginning to dry and is turning from yellow to red. It is usually thrown away with the husk as useless. This is a waste of beneficial plant matter, because it is not useless – corn silk is one of our favourite herbs, not only because it makes a pleasant and effective tea, but because the sweetcorn, which contains appreciable amounts of vitamin B6, can be eaten as well.

Buy the sweetcorn as fresh and succulent as possible, collect the silk from each corn cob and spread it out on a tray to dry. This process takes only a day or two. Store in strong brown paper bags in a cool place. To make the tea, chop roughly and use 1 teaspoon to a cup of boiling water. The tea can be drunk either hot or cold.

Corn silk is a soothing diuretic, used to gently promote urination. It is also calming. It soothes and heals the kidneys, improving their function, and can therefore help in many conditions where good elimination is important. One or two cups of corn silk tea taken during the day will alleviate many cases of bedwetting. For kidney pains and chronic cystitis, make an extra-strong tea by using 2 teaspoons of herb per cup, and drink three cups a day. Corn silk is also used to flush gravel and stones from the kidneys; because it promotes good kidney function it will often succeed where other diuretics fail.

## CORNMEAL MUSH
### Serves 4

150 g/5 oz/1 cup cornmeal
1 tsp salt
250 ml/8 fl oz/1 cup cold water
800 ml/1⅓ pints/3⅓ cups boiling water

*Mix the corn, salt and cold water together. Place the boiling water in the top of a water bath and gradually add the corn mixture. Cook and stir the mush over a high heat for 2–3 minutes, then cover and steam for 15 minutes.*

## CORNFLOUR (CORNSTARCH) PUDDING

*Cornflour (cornstarch) was a frequent ingredient in invalid food, especially in the last century. This recipe serves 2–4*

15 g/½ oz/2 tablespoons cornflour (cornstarch)
300 ml/½ pint/1¼ cups cow's, soya or almond milk
1½ teaspoons cane sugar or honey
flavouring as desired
1 egg, separated

*Mix the cornflour (cornstarch) into a smooth paste with a little of the milk. Put the remaining milk in a saucepan and heat, add the cornflour (cornstarch) and stir constantly until the mixture boils and thickens. Simmer for at least 5 minutes. Remove from the heat and add the sugar, flavourings (if used) and the egg yolk. Beat the white of egg to a stiff froth and fold it into the mixture. Quickly pour into a greased pie dish and bake in a preheated oven at 180°C/350°F/Gas Mark 4 until browned and risen, about 20 minutes. Serve immediately with cream or stewed fruit if wished.*

## CORN WATER

*This is a good remedy for nausea and vomiting. Makes 200 ml/7 fl oz/⅞ cup*

150 g/5 oz/1 cup fresh sweetcorn kernels
900 ml/1½ pints/3¾ cups water

*Spread the corn out on a baking tray and put in the oven at 120°C/250°F/Gas Mark ½ or lower until the corn is 'parched' and dehydrated. The time this takes depends on the heat and the freshness of the corn. Put the parched corn into a pan, add the water and make into a decoction. Reduce to 200 ml/7 fl oz/⅞ cup. Dose: 1 teaspoon when needed. 1–3 teaspoons in a cup of water can be drunk freely.*

# Zingiber officinale
# Ginger

This highly aromatic root with a hot, sweet flavour is available in many forms: dried and ground, fresh, crystallized (candied), preserved in syrup or used in wines, cordials and ginger beer.

Ginger root is the knobbly rhizome of a tall, reed-like perennial plant grown in the tropics. It needs a constant, hot, humid climate and heavy rainfall. It has been cultivated since early times in India and South-East Asia and is still considered to be essential to the daily diet there to protect against diseases and aid digestion. It is mentioned by Confucius (551–478BC) and in the Koran and was one of the first true spices to be brought to Europe by Arab traders. The Romans are reputed to have introduced ginger to Britain.

Medicinally, ginger is used to stimulate digestion, reduce nausea and ease flatulence. It has antiseptic qualities and is a useful expectorant, loosening phlegm and clearing catarrh. It is a warming antispasmodic, relaxing from the inside, and is excellent for curing and preventing chills or as a pick-me-up when tense, cold and exhausted. It stimulates the immune system, giving the body an extra boost – 'gingering up the system'. It is often included with other herbs to round off a remedy and generate a sense of total well-being.

In Ayurvedic medicine ginger is the 'universal medicine'. Fresh ginger juice and ground ginger are pounded into a paste, rolled into pea-sized pills and dried. Two pills are taken three times a day. In China it is used as a tonic for potency and longevity and as an aphrodisiac.

Ginger is a major ingredient in antispasmodic hot oils and rubs. A ten-minute massage with infused ginger oil will ease tired muscles, clear toxins, relax muscle spasm and cramps, relieve aching joints, improve circulation and diminish pain in general. A warm compress applied to the abdomen will relax menstrual cramps and heavy drawing pains.

Chew ginger to cure travel sickness, nausea in pregnancy and toothache, and to clear the head and unblock sinuses.

## GINGER PANCAKES

These are delicious with honey and yogurt.
Makes about 25 pancakes

90 g/3½ oz/⅞ cup flour
1 teaspoon ground ginger
pinch of salt
250 ml/8 fl oz/1 cup milk or water
3 teaspoons rum or brandy
1 egg, separated

Mix all the ingredients except the egg white together until smooth. Allow to stand for 1 hour. Just before use, beat the egg white until stiff and then fold into the batter. Cook a tablespoonful at a time on a hot griddle.

## GINGER ALE

This adapted version of ginger beer is a digestive aid.
Makes 600 ml/1 pint/2½ cups

7.5 cm/3 inch piece of ginger root, grated
600 ml/1 pint/2½ cups boiling water
15 ml/1 tablespoon honey
carbonated mineral water

Add the ginger root to the water and simmer for 20 minutes in a covered pan. Strain, cool and store in the refrigerator. To drink, add carbonated water to taste.

## TRUE GINGER BEER
Makes 4½ litres/8 pints/5 quarts

4½ litres/8 pints/5 quarts boiling water
1 lemon, sliced
25 g/1 oz ginger root, chopped, or 1 tablespoon ground ginger
450 g/1 lb/2 cups sugar
15 g/½ oz fresh yeast
1 slice toast

Pour the water over the lemon, ginger and sugar and stir until the sugar dissolves. Spread the yeast on the toast and add to the liquid when it is lukewarm. Stand for 12 hours in a warm place. Strain and bottle. Tie or cork down securely and put in a cool place. This is ready to drink in a week's time.

# Salt

Salt is one of the most basic and common commodities. Alchemists regarded it as one of the three major elements, with sulphur and quicksilver (mercury). Three-quarters of the world is saline oceans and we each contain our own internal sea. Yet salt is very valuable, hence the saying that people are 'worth their salt'. Salt regulates the tides and internal flow of water in and around our cells. It can save lives. The body can lose salt through chronic diarrhoea, dehydration, shock and loss of blood, but long-term deficiencies are unlikely as salt is put into most manufactured food – in fact most people take too much salt.

## SALT BATHS

*The body eliminates waste from the system through the lungs, bowel, bladder and skin. A salt bath draws impurities out through the skin by osmotic pressure. Add ½–1 cup of sea salt to your bath and soak in it for at least 20 minutes to gain the full benefit. Rinse your body with plenty of clean water. Use for toxic, retaining conditions (when the body feels 'full' and stagnant), tiredness, stiffness and after flu to cleanse the system.*

## SOMA'S EXOTIC SALT BATH AND SCRUB

*1 tablespoon bicarbonate of soda*
*5 drops essential oil*
*juice of 1 lemon*
*1 teaspoon good oil, such as sweet almond*
*100 g/4 oz/½ cup sea salt*

*Stir the bicarbonate of soda, essential oil, lemon juice and oil together and then blend in the salt. Dissolve in the bath water.*

*The skin has balanced microflora so it is best not to use this scrub often, but a whole body scrub is a good spring ritual; it removes dead skin cells, clears pores and tones blood circulation to the skin. Rub all over, rinse with cold water, towel dry and wrap up warm.*

## SIMPLE TOOTH POWDER

*1 teaspoon ground fresh sage*
*6 teaspoons sea salt*

*Grind the sage and salt together in a pestle and mortar until thoroughly combined. Pour into a clean 30 ml jar and pack down tightly.*
*To use: Put a small amount on to a toothbrush and brush in the usual way. Rinse your mouth with plenty of water.*

## ZINGY TOOTHPASTE

*1 teaspoon fresh sage, ground*
*6 teaspoons sea salt*
*1 teaspoon bicarbonate of soda*
*¼ teaspoon ground cloves (optional)*

*Grind all the ingredients together in a pestle and mortar until they form a fine powder. Pour into a clean 30 ml jar and pack down tightly.*
*To use: Put a small amount on to a toothbrush and brush in the usual way. Rinse your mouth with plenty of water. If you have sore gums, add cloves to act as an analgesic.*

Salt accentuates flavours, energy and sharpness, makes tastes more pointed and more fiery. Just as salt accentuates flavours it also accentuates emotions. In traditional Indian medicine it feeds fire, leading to stress and high blood pressure. People with a history of high blood pressure should avoid salt in their diet. In small amounts it is soothing.

A very strong saline solution acts as both an emetic and purgative. A very weak one softens water and is the most balanced, least disturbing substance that can be applied to the skin, as it is cooling, antiseptic and cleansing. When diluted at the strength of 'thin tears', it can be used to wash even the most delicate parts of the body, for example the eyes. Although gentle, it is also thorough and strong, cleaning gums and throat, wounds and so on. However, although it is a nourisher, salt also kills; salting the ground prevents plants from growing and can turn meadows into barren wastes. A lesson to avoid excess, even in good things!

# Honey

Whole books are devoted to the properties, complexities and virtues of honey. It contains all the sustenance for bees – energy, enzymes, minerals and trace elements. Always use single, unblended honey as it takes on some of the qualities of the plants from which the pollen is gathered.

## EMERGENCY FLUID

*The sugars in honey are predigested, making them easily available as energy to a weakened body. This soothing drink replaces valuable fluids in infective diarrhoea and vomiting. Drink freely.*

1 teaspoon honey
¼ teaspoon salt
300 ml/½ pint/1¼ cups pure water

## COUGH SYRUPS

*These recipes use the antiseptic, demulcent and expectorant qualities of the honey to preserve the herbs and facilitate their action. Use fresh or dried herbs.*

Basic formula for restlessness and slight fever:
25 g/1 oz chamomile
4 cloves garlic or 6 cloves
juice of ½ lemon
5 cm/2 inch piece ginger root, grated
pinch of cayenne pepper
450 g/1 lb/2 cups sugar

*Make as for thyme syrup (see page 40). The chamomile can be reduced and any of the following substituted according to need:*
2–4 teaspoons thyme in unproductive cough
2 teaspoons sage for sore throat
6 teaspoons sage for fevers
5 cm/2 inches cinnamon stick or 1 teaspoon ground cinnamon for a cold and runny nose
2 teaspoons aniseed for wheeziness
1 small onion for dry cough
4 teaspoons fennel seed for bronchial catarrh

*For children, make as above but use half the amount of herbs.*

Dose: 1 teaspoon 3–4 times a day, or every 2 hours. Reduce the dosage proportionally for children under 10 and mix with a little water.

## BRAIN 'MEAD'

*This elixir of life strengthens the brain and memory, keeps the blood thin, blood pressure balanced, nerves strong and circulation prime. It also encourages the appetite and gratifies the stomach. In olden times, this strong tonic would have been made with mead, a fermented honey drink. This recipe could also be turned into a tincture or a tonic wine.*

50 g/2 oz rosemary, fresh or dried
2 tablespoons sage, fresh or dried
1 tablespoon basil, fresh or dried
1 tablespoon parsley, fresh or dried
4 teaspoons fennel seeds, crushed
4 garlic cloves, crushed (optional)
2 teaspoons ground ginger or 1 teaspoon cayenne pepper
juice of 2 lemons and 5 cm/2 inches peel
20 cloves
6 cardamom pods (optional)
1.75 litres/3 pints/7½ cups water
450 g/1 lb honey

*Make all the ingredients except the honey into a decoction. Reduce the liquid to 300 ml/½ pint/1¼ cups before adding the honey (see page 40).*
Dose: 1 teaspoon 2–4 times a day.

## HONEY POULTICE

*Honey is antiseptic and drawing. This action can be used to draw poisons or clean infected wounds. It was used to clean wounds in the First World War. If the honey is too thin, thicken it with cornflour (cornstarch). A thick layer is needed to draw effectively. Once the wounds are clean, honey acts as a healer. Garlic honey can be applied directly to small wounds.*

Linden is a relaxing honey, clover a strengthening tonic, heather wild and strong with a tinge of melancholy. Honey is soothing, demulcent, antiseptic, expectorant and healing.

# Oils

Two types of oils are obtained from plants: fixed oils and volatile oils. Fixed oils are found in nuts and seeds and are obtained by pressing. Volatile (or essential) oils are the aromatic fragrance of the plant, found in oil glands on flowers, leaves, bark and roots. They are usually obtained by distilling over a solvent.

The cost of essential oils varies hugely and reflects the quality of the oil and the manner of extraction. Good-quality essential oils are expensive. They are also very strong and must be diluted before use. Fortunately, it is easy to make good-quality infused oils from aromatic plants. These don't need diluting and reflect more of the whole qualities of the plant than do essential oils.

Fixed oils should be as fresh and as near to the original state as possible, which is to say they should be cold-pressed, not heated, solidified or emulsified.

## Oil for skin

For the face it is best to use an oil which has some therapeutic power in its own right, for example sweet almond oil, which is soothing and nourishing. Wheatgerm oil is rich in vitamin E, excellent for the skin and for fragile capillaries, but it is a strong-smelling oil and is best used in small amounts to enrich or preserve a lighter oil. Sunflower, peanut, safflower and grapeseed are all useful. They are light, colourless and relatively odourless. Oils used for making herbal infused oils should be light enough not to drown the fragrance of the herbs.

All fixed oils oxidize over time and become rancid. This can be delayed by adding 5–10 per cent of wheatgerm oil or 5 per cent of vitamin E oil.

## Oil in the diet

Certain types of oil, called essential fatty acids, are vital in the daily diet. They are used to make the walls of cells and a deficiency can cause a number of problems including premenstrual syndrome, painful breasts and dry eczema. They are found in leafy vegetables, oily fish and cold-pressed vegetable oils. Evening primrose oil is an especially rich source which can be used internally and externally to give relief in dry skin conditions. Taken daily, it is beneficial for arthritic conditions.

---

## GEOFF'S CHEST OIL

*This chest rub is for dry, irritable and infected coughs, chest tightness, shoulder tension and asthma. If there are asthmatic children in the house it is worth while making this to keep on hand. Rub it all over the chest, front and back, especially between the shoulder blades, before bed.*

*8 g/¼ oz dried thyme*
*8 g/¼ oz dried lavender*
*8 g/¼ oz dried aniseed*
*3 garlic cloves, crushed or 1 onion, sliced*
*10 cloves (optional)*
*1 chamomile teabag (optional if excessively restless)*
*pinch of ground ginger (optional if cold or chilled)*
*300 ml/½ pint/1¼ cups vegetable oil*

*Make into an infused oil (see page 31), bottle and label. It can also be thickened and used as a plaister (see page 37).*

---

## SALVES

*Animal fats such as butter, goose grease and bear's fat were the traditional carriers for herbal ointments and salves in still-room books. The herbs were infused into the fats in the same way as they are infused into the oils. When the fats cooled they naturally became a solid cream. Strained vegetable shortening can be used as a substitute.*
*'Mix 2 parts of honey with 1 part lard or goose grease. Put a little on the ladle of a spoon and place right at the back of the throat, it will dissolve slowly and loosen tightness.'*

A traditional English recipe

# Vinegar

Vinegar is used in many diets as a cleanser and regulator. Many people drink cider vinegar (or a spiced herbal vinegar) and warm water first thing in the morning. This keeps the skin clear and the system toned and regular. A large number of people also find this regime helpful for rheumatism and arthritis. Because vinegar is a bacterial reaction and not a yeast fermentation it is an ideal bath or douche for thrush and various itches.

Externally, vinegar is cooling and antiseptic. The weak acid will neutralize insect and wasp bites and alter the pH of the skin, killing fungal infections like athlete's foot and thrush and preventing further trouble. It is soothing for irritable skin conditions and burns, including sunburn. A cold compress – it does not have to be iced – will draw out heat, reduce swellings and speed healing. Dilute vinegar also makes an excellent hair rinse to keep the hair shiny and soothe an irritable scalp.

Vinegar can be made from wine, sherry, cider, malt and rice. (On pages 24–7 you will find recipes for making cider, wine, fruit and spiced vinegars.) It is widely employed in the

## HOME-MADE BALSAMIC VINEGAR

*6 green cardamom pods*
*12 sultanas (golden raisins) or raisins*
*12 black peppercorns*
*1 teaspoon sage*
*1 teaspoon rosemary*
*4 cloves*
*300 ml/¹/₂ pint/1¹/₄ cups cider vinegar*

*Macerate all the ingredients together for 2 months, then strain and bottle. Experiment with various combinations of herbs and spices.*
*To use: This vinegar can be used in cooking and salad dressings. To use as a drink, tonic, stimulant, balancer, cooler, skin wash, cooling lotion, compress or hair rinse, dilute 1 tsp vinegar in 250 ml/8 fl oz/1 cup water (hot or iced).*

## AUNTY HELEN'S PICCALILLI

Makes 1.8 kg/4 lb

*1 large cauliflower, broken into 2.5 cm/1 inch florets*
*2 cucumbers, cut into 1 cm/¹/₂ inch cubes*
*1 kg/2 lb shallots, sliced*
*1 kg/2 lb apples (dessert or cooking), cut into 1 cm/¹/₂ inch cubes*
*a brine of 450 g/1 lb salt dissolved in 4.5 litres/8 pints/5 quarts water*
*25 g/1 oz chilli peppers*
*50 g/2 oz garlic cloves*
*25 g/1 oz root ginger, bruised*
*25 g/1 oz black peppercorns*
*2.2 litres/4 pints/10 cups vinegar*
*50 g/2 oz cornflour (cornstarch)*
*25 g/1 oz turmeric*
*25 g/1 oz mustard powder*

*Cover the vegetables and fruit with cold brine and stand overnight. Drain and pack into hot sterilized jars. Boil the whole spices in vinegar for 5 minutes. Blend the cornflour (cornstarch), turmeric and mustard with a little cold vinegar, then stir into the boiling vinegar and boil for 10 minutes. Pour over the vegetables, filling the jars, and seal once cool. Store in a cool dark place. This piccalilli is best after 6 weeks. It keeps indefinitely, but refrigerate it once opened.*

## APPLE MINT VINEGAR

*250 ml/8 fl oz/1 cup apple juice*
*pinch of ground cinnamon*
*¹/₂ teaspoon chopped mint*
*1 tablespoon cider vinegar*

*Mix the ingredients together and pour into a glass containing crushed ice. This can be diluted with water to taste.*

making of pickles. In piccalilli (a traditional British pickle), it preserves the minerals and vitamins of the fresh vegetables, and the vinegar promotes digestion while the spices add stimulative warmth. In general, it is a 'good medicine', giving real balancing nourishment. There are many different recipes, the above being an unusual one in that it is sugarless.

# Wines, Beers and Spirits

In the Bible, Paul the Apostle advises his disciple Timothy to 'Use a little wine for the sake of your stomach and your frequent cases of sickness.' Such quotes were often used to counter-balance the religious abstinence of the Temperance Movement. Verses can also be found to condemn the excessive use of wine. Moderation in all things! Recent research has shown that a little red wine is good for the heart. Excessive wine is, of course, bad for the liver.

Many people are allergic to wine, or to the additives and chemicals in it. Red wine especially can bring on headaches and allergic rashes. It is worth trying organic wine, since it may be the chemicals that cause the upset. Alternatively, try making your own, using the best quality natural ingredients.

There is not enough room here to explore the making of herbal wines, but many good books are available. Making infused wines by steeping herbs in good-quality grape wine is a reasonable compromise. Tonics, digestives and aperitifs can all be made this way.

Beers are simple to make and nutritive to drink. Herb beers can be made by preparing a decoction (see page 18) and following the recipe for ginger beer on page 80.

## BILL'S TONIC WINE RECIPE

*1 bottle of wine of reasonable quality*
*sprig of fresh thyme*
*½ nutmeg, grated*
*1 cm/½ inch ginger root, grated*
*1 cinnamon stick*
*8 large raisins*

*Pour a little of the wine from the bottle, add the herbs and recork. Leave to stand for 2 weeks. Strain and replace in the bottle. Cork and label.*
*To use: Take ½ a small wineglass full, with water if preferred, whenever in need of a little uplifting. Experiment with your own mixtures of herbs, but don't try to make the tonic wine stronger by adding larger amounts as this would spoil the flavour.*

## HERBAL DIGESTIVE TONIC

*Makes 250 ml/8 fl oz/1 cup*

*20 green cardamom seeds, crushed*
*1 teaspoon fennel seeds, crushed*
*1 teaspoon dried rosemary*
*zest of ½ lemon*
*zest of ½ orange*
*5 cm/2 inches cinnamon stick*
*10 cloves (optional)*
*1 teaspoon poppy seeds (optional)*
*10 sultanas (golden raisins) (optional)*
*250 ml/8 fl oz/1 cup vodka or other spirits*

*Steep the herbs, fruit and spices in the alcohol for 2 weeks, shaking occasionally. Strain and bottle. You can add other herbs and spices or nuts and dried fruit to make your own distinctive digestive tonic.*

*To use: Take 1–2 teaspoons in a little water before meals, or when needed to settle the stomach. This keeps for over a year, by which time it will be long drunk!*

Beers are cooling and refreshing in hot weather, while spirits and spiced wines are warming, good in cold weather and, as old herbals say, 'grateful to the stomach'. Alcohol is an appetizer in its own right, but more so if turned into an aperitif, with aromatic bitter herbs such as juniper and rosemary. Hot brandy taken before bed is diaphoretic and helps to break a fever.

Used externally, tinctures and wines are antiseptic and tend to dry and harden the skin. Thyme tincture, for example, can be used as an aftershave or an astringent lotion.

# Herb Chart

| | Acidity | Anxiety | Aphrodisiacs | Arthritis | Bad Breath | Breast Pain | Circulation | Colds | Colic & Flatulence | Constipation | Coughs | Cystitis | Depression | Diarrhoea |
|---|---|---|---|---|---|---|---|---|---|---|---|---|---|---|
| **SPICES** | | | | | | | | | | | | | | |
| Aniseed | | | T, Tr | T, Tr, G | | | | | T, Tr | | T | | T, Tr, M | |
| Cardamom | | | | | | | | | T, Tr | | | | T, Tr | |
| Cayenne | | | | O, M, Pl | | | T, Tr, M, O | | | | | | | |
| Cinnamon | | | T, Tr | | | | T, Tr | T, Tr, I | T, Tr | | | | | T |
| Cloves | | | T, Tr, I | O, M | | | | | T, Tr | | M + Thyme | In herb teas | | |
| Fennel | | T, Tr | | T, Tr, O, M | | T, Tr, C | | | T, Tr | | T | T + barley | T, Tr, M | |
| Ginger | | | T, Tr, B | O, M, B | | | T, Tr, M, O | T, Tr, I | T, Tr | | | | | |
| Juniper | | | | T, O, M, B | T | | M | | | | | T + barley | | |
| **HERBS** | | | | | | | | | | | | | | |
| Chamomile | T | T, M, B | | | | C | | | T, Tr, P, C | T | | | | T |
| Corn silk | | | | | | T | | | | | | T | | |
| Marigold | T | | | | | T, Tr, C | T | T | T | | | | T | |
| Parsley | | | | T | T, G, E | T | T | | | | | T | | |
| Peppermint | | | T, Tr | | | | | T, I | T, Tr | | | | | |
| Rosemary | | | | T, Tr, O, M | | | T, Tr, M, O | | T, Tr | | | | T, Tr, B | |
| Sage | | | | T, Tr, C, M, V | | T, Tr, C | | T | | T | | T | T, Tr, M | |
| Thyme | | | | T, M | | | | | T | | T, S, M, Pl | T + barley | | |
| **OTHER** | | | | | | | | | | | | | | |
| Barley | Water | | | | | | | | Water | | Water | Water | | |
| Cabbage | T, J | | | P, E | | P | | | | E | | | | |
| Carrot | J, Soup | | | | | P | | | | E | | | | J, Soup |
| Cucumber | | | | | | | | | | | | | | |
| Figs | | | | | | | | | | | S, E | S | | |
| Garlic | | | | | | | E | T, S, E | | | S, M | | | E |
| Honey | | In herb teas | | | | | | | | | In herb teas | | In herb teas | |
| Lemon | In water | | | J | | | J, in teas | In herb teas | | | With honey | In herb teas | | + carrots |
| Oats | T | E | | P | | | E | | | E | | | E | |
| Onion | | | | | | | E | T, S, E | | | S, M | | | |
| Salt | | | | B | | | | | | | | | | With sugar |
| Vinegar | In water | | | | | | | | | | | | | |

This chart is a quick reference to the many properties and uses of the different herbs, spices and other ingredients described in the book. The key to the abbreviations used is as follows:

| | | | | | |
|---|---|---|---|---|---|
| B  Bath | E  Eaten | I  Inhalant | L  Lotion | O  Ointment | PL Plaister | T  Tea | V  Vinegar |
| C  Compress | G  Gargle | J  Juice | M  Massage oil | P  Poultice | S  Syrup | TR Tincture | W  Wash |

| | Earache | Eczema | Sore Eyes | Fevers | Fungal Infection | Hair Care | Headaches | Insomnia | Menopause | Mouth Care | Period Pain | Sinusitis | Sore Throat | Spots & Acne |
|---|---|---|---|---|---|---|---|---|---|---|---|---|---|---|
| **SPICES** | | | | | | | | | | | | | | |
| ANISEED | | | | | | | | T | | | | | | |
| CARDAMOM | | | | | | | T, TR | | | | | | | |
| CAYENNE | M | | | | | | | | | W + sage | M, O | | G + sage | |
| CINNAMON | | | | | | | | | | | | T, I | | |
| CLOVES | | | | | W | | | HOW?? | | W | HOW?? | | | |
| FENNEL | | | W, C, T | | | | | | T | | | | | |
| GINGER | | | | | | C, O, T | | | | | T, TR, C, B | T, M | | |
| JUNIPER | | | | | | | | | | | | | | W, L |
| **HERBS** | | | | | | | | | | | | | | |
| CHAMOMILE | | T, TR, L, W, O | W, C | T, W | V | W | T, TR, C | T, M, B | | | | T, I | | |
| CORN SILK | | | | | | | | | | | | | | |
| MARIGOLD | T | T, TR, L, W, O | W, C, O, T | T, W | T, TR, L, W, O | | | | | T | T, W | T, TR | T, G | T |
| PARSLEY | | T, W | | | | | | | T, Soup | | E | | | P |
| PEPPERMINT | | W | | T | | | C | T | | | T | T, I | | |
| ROSEMARY | | | | W | | T, TR, L, O, V | T, TR, C | | | | | | | |
| SAGE | | T | | T | | W | | | T, TR, B | T, G | | T, I | T, G | T, TR, W, L |
| THYME | | | | | L, W, V | | | T | | | | | G | |
| **OTHER** | | | | | | | | | | | | | | |
| BARLEY | | W | | Water | | | | | | | | | G | |
| CABBAGE | | | | | | | | | | | | | P | |
| CARROT | | | | | | | | | | E | | | | |
| CUCUMBER | | | C | W | | | | | | | | | | |
| FIGS | | | | | | | | | | | | | | |
| GARLIC | J, Oil | | | | J, O, V | | | | | | | T, E | | J |
| HONEY | | L | | | | | | in herb teas | | | | | G + lemon | |
| LEMON | | | | | | | | | | | | in herb teas | G + honey | J |
| OATS | | W, P | | | | | | | E | | | | | W, P |
| ONION | J, Oil, P | | | | | | | | | | | T, E | | J |
| SALT | | | W | | | | | | | G, Tooth pdr | | W | G | |
| VINEGAR | | | | W | W | W | W, C | | | W | | | G | W |

# Treating Everyday Conditions

The best medicine is preventative medicine. Adopt a good regime which includes a sensible diet with plenty of fresh vegetables, suitable exercise and time for relaxation. Remember that everyone is different, and that what suits your friends may not necessarily suit you. Take advice on the best regime for you and, above all, pay attention to your own body, to its unique needs. When you are ill, ask yourself what factors in your lifestyle may have led to the illness. Consider all your signs and symptoms, as they are often related. Headaches, for example, may be linked to digestive upsets, to catarrhal conditions, to neck tension or eye strain. Choose remedies which treat all the possible factors.

If the symptoms are new to you, or if they don't start to respond to treatment within a few days, get them checked out by your doctor or health professional. This book is designed to be of help for low-grade chronic (ongoing) complaints or for minor acute complaints. There is no substitute for expert advice.

For dosages, check the individual recipes.

**Arthritis and rheumatism (aches and pains in joints and muscles)** For longstanding aches and stiffness, apply warming rubs and plaisters and take baths using herbs such as ginger, cayenne, black pepper, fennel and rosemary. Drink sage or fennel tea regularly. To calm inflamed joints, apply a cabbage poultice or sage compress. Juniper and salt baths are always helpful. For aching feet, use mustard foot baths.

**Asthma** Asthma can be life-threatening and should always be assessed by a professional. It can be triggered by chest infections, allergies or nervous tension.

Asthma that is related only to coughs and colds can be helped by regular intake of garlic, combined with chest rubs as needed. A tea made from two parts of chamomile to one part of aniseed is helpful for either allergic or nervous asthma. Inhale the steam from the same mixture for quicker relief.

Allergies can include feathers, dust mites, pollen (see Hay Fever), cow's milk and sulphur dioxide (used as a preservative for wine and dried fruit).

**Bladder problems** Drink barley water. For cystisis, make it with fennel, thyme or juniper tea. Juniper is the strongest; use it with care. For an irritable bladder, drink plenty of plain barley water or corn silk tea.

**Children's ailments** Chamomile tea is the best general remedy. It can be used for teething troubles, insomnia, restlessness, nightmares, loss of appetite and as an aid in treating fevers. For infants, use two or three teaspoons of the tea in any drink. Add two cloves to the tea for extra effect, if needed.

**Coughs** Choose your medicine according to the type of cough. For a dry, irritating cough use soothing remedies such as onion syrup or barley water. For a loose, chesty cough, or if the phlegm is stuck, use thyme tea with honey and lemon, or thyme syrup. Thyme is also good for a tight chest and wheeziness.

Examine the phlegm coughed up. If it is white or grey, these methods should be sufficient. Pale yellow indicates infection; use garlic and garlic oil or thyme oil chest rubs. Seek professional help for persistent dark yellow or green phlegm or for persistent dry coughs.

Some people are very prone to coughs. Colds always 'go straight to their chest'. In these cases strengthen the lungs with sage or thyme tea, taken 2 or 3 cups a day for three months.

**Depression and lethargy** The best teas are fennel, rosemary, sage and cardamom, mixed according to taste. Back these up with baths and massages using infused oils of the same herbs or with infused oil of rose petals. For low libido use ginger, cloves, peppermint, cinnamon or aniseed in wines, teas and baths.

**Digestive troubles** Think carefully about what brings the symptoms on. Is it stress or diet, or a combination of both? Keep a diet diary, writing down everything eaten or drunk over one week, noting any change in stress levels or symptoms. This will often pinpoint areas in your life that need changing. If there seems to be a sensitivity to a particular food or drink, then try a challenge test. Cut it out for four weeks and then reintroduce it. If the challenge makes the symptoms worse, try a longer period without that particular food. Only test one food at a time. DON'T MAKE BIG CHANGES IN YOUR DIET WITHOUT CONSULTING A NUTRITIONIST – it is easy to finish up with a diet that is deficient in essential nutrients.

Chamomile tea is a great help for all digestive problems. For weak digestion, take rosemary tea or wine with spices. For heartburn and acidity, take one teaspoon of lemon juice or cider vinegar in a cup of warm water. Cabbage water, barley water and carrot juice or soup are very soothing.

*For wind and colic,* use spices in cooking. Drink fennel, aniseed, cardamom or peppermint tea. Drink ginger or cardamom decoctions to cure nausea. For diarrhoea, take lemon juice with carrot juice or soup. Use garlic for intestinal infections, and take salt and sugar if the diarrhoea goes on for too long.

*For constipation,* eat plenty of fruit and whole grain cereals. Take fig syrup and make sure you get plenty of exercise, especially if your work is largely sedentary.

*For liverishness,* take rosemary, marigold or lemon juice in warm water.

*For hiccoughs,* take neat vinegar with a pinch of brown sugar or fresh mint tea.

*For cases of thread worms,* strong thyme tea with lemon juice or garlic taken before breakfast for two weeks running will often effect a cure.

**Ear ache** Drop a little garlic oil into the ear. For chronic ear aches, rub the ear twice daily with a cayenne-based massage oil. For wax, shake together lemon juice and oil, drop this in the ear and plug with cotton wool. Never poke anything into your ears.

**Elderly people's ailments** Smaller doses of the herbs may be needed. Most older people will benefit from adding a little cayenne to their teas, tinctures and so on to rebalance the circulation and warm the digestion.

**Exhaustion, stress and anxiety** The most obvious causes of exhaustion are stresses at home or work, including emotional stresses. Dealing with stress is an art that can be acquired. Physical exercise is important for burning off excess adrenalin; employ relaxation techniques such as visualizations, yoga, meditation, walks in the countryside and listening to music or tapes designed to aid relaxation. Drink chamomile tea daily, not only to deal with immediate stress and anxiety but also to build up resistance.

Oats, sage, rosemary, aniseed and fennel seed are all good pick-me-ups and better in the long-term than stimulants such as coffee. A spoonful of good-quality honey will add to the restorative action of herbal teas. For insomnia and restless sleep, drink double-strength chamomile tea about an hour before bed, adding two or three cloves for extra effectiveness. Herbal pillows are also useful.

For exhaustion following an illness, drink three or four cups of sage or marigold tea daily and have sage or rosemary baths. Cold sage tea is effective for night sweats. Sage, marigold, garlic and ginger may be used, together or separately, for throwing off recurrent infections. Parsley drinks and salads are best for anaemia.

**Eyes** For sore eyes or conjunctivitis, use a wash or compress of fennel, chamomile or marigold tea, well strained and with a little salt added. Slices of cucumber are very soothing. Marigold ointment is the best remedy for dry or itchy eyes and eyelids. Fennel and marigold have a reputation for strengthening the eyesight. Apply a little onion juice to styes, being careful not to get it into the eye.

**Fevers** Always consult your doctor about a fever. If it is a minor infection, drinking a cup of sage or marigold tea every few hours will speed recovery. Cooling washes, made from cucumbers, rosemary tea or vinegar in water, will help keep temperature down and alleviate irritable rashes. For feverish chills, drink ginger and cinnamon decoction.

**Hay fever** This can be alleviated by taking a teaspoonful of local honey three times daily.

**Headaches** Try to pin down the cause, or causes, of your headache. Some people are especially prone to headaches arising from a number of different causes.

Tension headaches often start in the neck and feel like a tight band. They may be due to stress, poor posture, badly designed seating, carrying heavy weights and so on. Sinus pain is felt around the eyes and is usually associated with colds or a build up of mucus (see Nose and sinuses, below).

Chamomile is the best herbal tea for headaches in general. Combine it with rosemary if the headache feels cold, is worse in the cold, comes with failing memory or with indigestion. Add cardamom in depression or exhausted states.

Back up the herbal teas with a compress of the same herbs. Lie down for 10 minutes with the compress on your forehead. A vinegar compress on the back of the neck will relieve headaches brought on by hot weather.

Seek professional help if the headaches come with a fever, follow a blow to the head (even if it was some time ago) or if they are steadily getting worse.

Chamomile tea and a compress with chamomile and lavender oil will provide some relief for migraine, but professional help is usually needed.

**Mouth and throat** Sage is the most useful herb for all disorders of the mouth and throat. Use a strong tea, for mouth washes and gargles, and mix it with salt for tooth powders. For a sore throat, add honey and lemon or a small pinch of cayenne, according to what feels best. If persistent, wrap a crushed cabbage leaf around the throat. For laryngitis, add a small pinch of mustard powder to the gargle. For bad breath with no obvious cause, see aniseed (page 75).

**Nose and sinuses** It is well worth trying three weeks without milk or milk products, since this often lies behind chronic blocked and runny noses or sinus pains. Peppermint and sage teas are helpful. Add chamomile if an allergy is suspected. Add cinnamon for rhinitis. Don't forget to inhale the healing vapours as you drink the hot tea. Take lemon juice daily and try a nasal wash with salt water. For sinus pain, massage a cayenne-based oil or ointment such as Non's Hot Oil (see page 61) over the painful area, taking care to avoid your eyes and washing your hands well afterwards.

To prevent colds, take garlic regularly. To prevent chills turning into colds, drink ginger and cinnamon decoction.

**Poor circulation** Rosemary tea, taken daily for some months, is the best long-term solution. Ginger and cinnamon are helpful in the short term. For particular areas of cold, such as cold feet, massage with rosemary or cayenne oils or sprinkle cayenne powder into your socks. Cayenne ointment will heal chilblains; if they are broken, use marigold ointment. Eat plenty of oats, barley, garlic, ginger and cayenne to combat high cholesterol levels in the blood. Garlic will also help high blood pressure, but these problems should be treated under guidance by a doctor or other health professional. Suitable exercise is an important part of the treatment of all circulatory problems.

**Scalp and hair** Rosemary is the best herb, taken internally as a tea, tincture or wine or used externally in lotions, oils or vinegars. Rosemary vinegar is applicable to most scalp problems including dandruff. Use the oil for dry scalps. Add marigold for spots and rashes. For premature baldness, try rosemary and ginger as a compress or massage oil and drink the tea as well.

**Skin problems** The most useful herb for all types of skin problem is marigold, taken as a tea and applied as a compress, lotion, wash, ointment or cream. It may be used with any of the following remedies.

*Acne and spots:* Eat plenty of fruit, drink plenty of water and avoid sweet foods and drinks. Use lemon juice or marigold tincture as lotions. Sage tea is a good lotion for greasy skins.

Oat washes will draw out the spots. For boils and abscesses use the same regime backed up with marigold tea and poultices made from marigolds, lightly cooked onions, fresh figs, barley flour or oats.

*Eczema and itchy rashes:* To soothe raw and weeping rashes use honey, strong chamomile tea, or barley water made with chamomile tea. Seek help if the rash gets infected. For itching in general, use oat or vinegar washes and baths. Strong peppermint tea is very cooling. Drink chamomile tea for nervousness and stress.

*Fungal infections:* Garlic will banish most fungal infections. It is worth putting up with the smell, but don't use it on broken skin. Thyme and marigold are both good anti-fungals. Use them powdered in baby talc for athlete's foot. Chamomile vinegar is useful for groin infections.

*Warts and veruccas:* Garlic or lemon juice or crushed garlic mixed with lemon peel can help to cure stubborn cases.

*Chapped and dry skin, wrinkles and broken veins:* These respond to Lemon Skin Balm (see page 64). Add a little glycerine for deep wrinkles. This mixture also works with corns.

**Varicose veins** Drink rosemary tea with lemon juice. Apply marigold ointment or use marigold compresses for inflamed areas of skin. Varicose ulcers should be treated by a professional.

**Women's health** *Painful periods:* Drink double-strength chamomile tea, adding three or four cloves or a little ginger if necessary. Also use the same tea as a bath or as a compress applied to the lower abdomen. Take marigold, chamomile or peppermint tea regularly for the two weeks beforehand in order to avoid tension building up.

*Premenstrual tension and painful breasts:* Drink sage and fennel tea and apply a compress or poultice of chamomile or marigold. For water retention, use parsley, juniper or corn silk. Parsley is also helpful for regulating periods.

*Vaginal thrush:* Make a bath or douche from garlic vinegar or marigold tea.

*Menopause:* Drink cold sage tea for hot flushes. Take oats and parsley for depression and general support.

*Nausea in pregnancy:* Drink ginger, lemon and honey tea.

*Birth:* Drink chamomile tea made with three or four cloves for a week or two before the birth. A salt and marigold bath helps healing afterwards.

*Breast feeding:* Fennel tea helps the milk flow and reduces colic. Weak fennel tea can also be given directly to the baby. For mastitis, try a carrot or cabbage poultice. Chamomile and marigold compresses are soothing and healing. Cold sage tea will help to dry up the milk flow if required.

# First Aid

## SAFETY FIRST

Most accidents happen in the home, so the first rule of first aid is to prevent accidents by making the home as safe as possible, especially when there are young children or old people about. Make sure medicines and household cleaning products are kept out of reach of children. Look around the home for other potentially dangerous areas – take a close look at stairs and the kitchen, for example. Make cots, high chairs, toys and so on as safe as possible. There are plenty of safety devices on the market: childproof boxes and bottles, stair gates, electric plug guards, fire guards, flex tidies and smoke alarms, to name but a few.

Attend a good first-aid class. Learn how the body functions and how you can use simple techniques for dealing effectively with household emergencies. Simple techniques, applied by trained individuals, save lives daily.

If an accident does occur, don't panic! Stop and take a deep breath or a drop of the Rescue Remedy from the Bach Flower Essences range to help you remain calm so that you may act more effectively.

## TAKING ACTION

**Bruises** A compress of vinegar or vinegar and brown paper poultice (page 28) should be applied to the bruise straight away. See under Aniseed (page 75) for a home-made remedy for contusions.

**Burns** The first thing to do is to remove as much heat as possible from the burn. Hold it in cold water or against an ice pack (a bag of frozen peas makes an excellent ice pack) for some minutes. To make sure that the burn heals quickly and well, apply neat lavender oil, butter, honey or marigold cream.

**Cuts** Clean the cut well in boiled water, salt water or marigold tincture. If the bleeding does not stop, sprinkle the cut with cayenne pepper or lemon juice. If the cut is deep or inflamed, make an antiseptic soak from six drops of lavender oil added to one cup of water. Soak the cut for at least 10 minutes then apply marigold cream or honey and cover with a clean bandage.

**Fainting/feeling faint** Lie down or put your head between your knees. Lavender or rosemary oil can be used instead of smelling salts. Rosemary tea is helpful.

**Insect bites and stings** Apply neat vinegar (especially good for wasp stings), marigold tincture, lavender tea or crushed parsley leaves. For bee stings, be sure to remove the sting first, either with tweezers or with a drawing poultice made from mashed onions or sodium bicarbonate. If you are allergic to stings and bites, apply a chamomile compress as soon as possible.

**Nose bleeds** Apply an iced-water compress to the back of the neck. If prone to nose bleeds, take a little lemon juice in water on a regular basis.

**Poisoning** Seek professional help. Remember to take the suspect substance, or a sample of the vomit, with you. For food poisoning, try to induce vomiting by sticking your finger down the patient's throat or giving an emetic drink made with a teaspoon each of mustard powder and salt in a glass of warm water. Do not use emetics for poisoning by chemicals as you could make the situation worse.

**Shock** Keep a general shock remedy such as the Rescue Remedy from the Bach Flower Essences range in the house and in the car for immediate first aid. Wrap up and keep warm. Give chamomile tea with honey. See under Aniseed (page 75) for how to make and use the Reviver mixture. This is worth making to keep on hand in the house.

**Sprains** Apply an ice pack, a vinegar compress or a crushed cabbage leaf as soon as possible and leave on until the swelling is reduced. Then rub in a warming cream or oil based on cayenne to restore the circulation and speed healing.

**Sunburn** Apply a compress of vinegar, cucumber juice or cold tea. Yogurt can be used as a cream. See under Lemon (page 64) for lemon and glycerine soothing lotion.

**Toothache** Chew a piece of ginger. Clove essential oil acts quickly, but for a sustained effect chew the cloves themselves.

# Family Health Chest

To safeguard your family's well-being, assemble a natural health chest. This is different from a medicine cabinet and needs a new way of thinking. Consider the personal health of your family. What are the commonest conditions that arise? Chest or stomach complaints, headaches or muscle aches? What type of colds are the norm? Make suitable remedies so that a treatment is always available. Do not wait until a condition is serious enough to warrant a visit to the doctor as this wastes healing time. Try to develop a constant awareness and respond promptly to any feelings of 'dis-ease' or being 'under the weather'. The aim is not to cure but to prevent disease and maintain a positive sense of well-being. Given time, most conditions are self-limiting, and the aim of home treatment is to help the body achieve and maintain a naturally healthy balance, reduce sickness time and make illness a less unpleasant experience. If there is no improvement, or the condition worsens, seek professional advice. Describe the symptoms and your treatment. If used as described, these remedies are compatible with orthodox drugs. Kitchen remedies will always help whatever the condition, even bringing comfort in terminal care.

One of the most important elements in kitchen remedies is the fact that they are made and administered by the family. Tender loving care is healing in its own right, a powerful therapy which is often underestimated. Use plenty.

*Salt, lemon or vinegar, garlic and honey are the most vital ingredients that are to be found in most houses. Collect together plaster, bandages, scissors, cotton wool, lint for compresses, tweezers for splinters and an eye bath. From a health food shop, buy some Rescue Remedy from the Bach Flower Essences range (or a similar remedy for shock), lavender essential oil and clove essential oil. Make, or buy, marigold cream or ointment and some marigold tincture. Make some of Non's Hot Oil (see page 61). Assemble all these ingredients and put in a well-marked box in an easily accessible place.*

Below is a suggestion for a health cupboard. Three items must be bought, the rest are home-made and based on the needs of the average family. Prepared items like the cough syrup, marigold tincture and Non's Hot Oil will keep indefinitely. Herbs deteriorate, so replace those not used each year.

**TO BUY**

1 **A shock remedy**, such as the Rescue Remedy from the Bach Flower Essences range. Use for any shock, accident or trauma. Speeds healing in humans and pets.

2 **Lavender essential oil** for burns, wounds, rashes, skin troubles. Use as an inhalant to reduce stress and headache and in a compress.

3 **Clove oil**, to act as an analgesic for toothache, sore gums and so on. Use 25 drops added to 25ml/1 fl oz/2 tablespoons oil for a good analgesic rub.

**TO MAKE**

1 **Marigold tincture** (see Tinctures, page 21). Use externally as an antiseptic lotion for spots, cuts and abrasions, and for compresses for swellings and sprains. Use internally to help the body deal with fever and to reduce inflammations.

2 **A general cough syrup** for coughs, colds, flu. It is a soothing expectorant and also relieves gastritis.
   **Timely relief syrup** (see page 40 for making syrups)
   *25 g/1 oz thyme*
   *6 cloves garlic*
   *15 g/½ oz cinnamon*
   *8 g/¼ oz aniseed*
   *1 teaspoon powdered ginger*
   *450 g/1 lb sugar or honey*
   *juice of ½ lemon (optional)*
   **Dose: Adult 1 teaspoon 3–4 times a day**

3 **A relaxing tea mix for adults** and children to help alleviate restlessness, fevers, teething, tummy upsets, etc.
   **Harmony tea**
   *25 g/1 oz chamomile*
   *15 g/½ oz cloves*
   *8 g/¼ oz aniseed (optional)*

4 **Garlic honey** (see page 43), as a soothing antiseptic and general herbal antibiotic. Dose: 1 teaspoon 3–6 times a day.

5 **Indigestion tea.** Take 1 cup after food to alleviate nausea, indigestion, wind and flatulence.
   **Calming heaven tea**
   *15 g/½ oz peppermint*
   *8 g/¼ oz fennel*
   *8 g/¼ oz parsley*
   *8 g/¼ oz chamomile for nervous stomach;*
      *or 15 g/½ oz for gastric upset (optional)*
   Brew for 4 minutes.

6 **A tonic to act as a restorative after illness,** when feeling run down and suffering from nervous exhaustion.
   **Nancy's pick-me-up**
   *25 g/1 oz sage*
   *10 g/⅓ oz basil*
   *8 g/¼ oz rosemary*
   *2 litres/3½ pints/12 cups wine*
   Mix the herbs and wine together and set the mixture to stand for 15 days in a cool place. Strain and bottle.
   **Dose: 1 wine glass (150 ml/¼ pint/⅔ cup) twice a day**

7 **Syrup of figs or prunes** (see page 69) for constipation

8 **Non's hot oil** (see page 61) for aches and pains, cramps, chilblains, muscle spasm, period pains

9 **Tea mix for women** to balance hormones and water retention, regulate periods and ease menopausal symptoms.
   **Women's way tea**
   *15 g/½ oz parsley*
   *15 g/½ oz sage*
   *8 g/¼ oz rosemary*
   Allow to brew for 4 minutes.
   **Dose: 1 cup 1–4 times a day when needed**

10 **A gargle for sore throats and gums**, loose teeth and tonsillitis. This can also be made into a tincture and diluted for use.
   **Sage saver mix**
   *25 g/1 oz sage*
   *1 tablespoon ground cloves*
   *1 tablespoon salt*
   **Dose: Gargle twice a day, or every 2 hours when needed**

11 **Chamomile balm.** This infused oil and beeswax cream is a soothing, nourishing antiseptic for chapped, dry and damaged skin. It is also good for rashes and allergic reactions.

# Glossary

The following terms are used to describe the properties of the herbs, spices and vegetables that appear in this book.

**Anaesthetic** An agent that numbs sensation and so reduces pain.
*Examples:* bay, clove.

**Analgesic** Has the effect of relieving pain.
*Examples:* nutmeg, pansy, willow.

**Anti-inflammatory** Reduces inflammation.
*Examples:* cabbage, cucumber, chamomile.

**Antiseptic** Kills bacteria and prevents infection.
*Examples:* Aniseed, cabbage, cayenne, chamomile, clove, garlic, honey, horseradish, juniper berries, lemon, marjoram, marigold, nutmeg, onion, parsley, peppermint, salt, turmeric, vinegar.

**Anti-spasmodic** Relieves spasms or cramps.
*Examples:* aniseed, caraway, coriander, ginger, horseradish, mustard seed, peppermint

**Astringent** Drying and contracting, reducing secretions.
*Examples:* lemon, sage, thyme,

**Carminative** Relaxes digestive tension and spasm. Reduces wind.
*Examples:* clove, coriander, fennel, parsley, peppermint, thyme.

**Decongestant** Relieves congestion.
*Examples:* horseradish, peppermint.

**Demulcent** Soothes irritated tissues, particularly mucous membranes.
*Examples:* barley, cucumber, honey.

**Depurative** Cleanses the blood.
*Examples:* garlic, onion.

**Diaphoretic** Promotes sweating.
*Examples:* brandy, cayenne, ginger, horseradish.

**Digestive** Aids digestion.
*Examples:* aniseed, barley, basil, bay, caraway, cardamom, carrots, chamomile, cinnamon, ginger, juniper berries, lettuce, marjoram, nutmeg, oats, rosemary, turmeric.

**Diuretic** Encourages urination.
*Examples:* corn silk, cucumber, fennel, juniper berries, lemon, parsley.

**Drawing** Draws poisons from boils and abcesses.
*Examples:* ginger, honey, oats.

**Emetic** Provokes vomiting.
*Examples:* nutmeg, salt.

**Expectorant** Expels sticky mucus from the lungs.
*Examples:* cloves, garlic, ginger, honey, marjoram, onion, thyme.

**Febrifuge** Helps to reduce fever.
*Examples:* chamomile, sage, yarrow.

**Hepatic** Strengthens the liver.
*Examples:* rosemary, turmeric.

**Rubefacient** A local irritant that causes reddening of the skin.
*Examples:* cayenne, mustard seed.

**Sedative** Calms the nerves.
*Examples:* chamomile, lettuce.

**Stimulant** Increases activity.
*Examples:* alcohol, basil, cayenne, cinnamon, nutmeg, peppermint, rosemary.

# Further Reading

Here are a few books that will be useful if you want to look at herbs in more detail:

Buchman, Dian: *Herbal Medicine: The Natural Way to Get Well and Stay Well* (Rider & Co., 1979 and 1983).
   A practical book with lots of personal experience, including family recipes. Excellent for beginners.

Buning, Frances, and Hambley, Paul: *Herbalism* (Headway Lifeguides, Hodder & Stoughton, 1993).
   An introduction to the theory and practice of herbal medicine, with helpful tips on using over-the-counter remedies.

Ody, Penelope: *The Herb Society's Complete Medicinal Herbal* (Dorling Kindersley, 1993).
   A complete guide to medicinal herbs and their uses, with photographs of each herb. It contains information on newly introduced Chinese herbs.

Smith, Keith Vincent: *The Illustrated Earth Garden Herbal: A Herbal Companion* (Thomas Nelson Australia Pty Ltd, 1978).
   A companion book of general interest which gives an overview to world of herbal medicine. It is illustrated with photographs of the most famous herbals.

Sources used in the book:

Bardswell, Frances A..: *The Herb Garden* (1911).
Cogan, Thomas: *The Haven of Health* (1584).
Coles, William: *The Art of Simpling* (London, 1656).
Culpeper, Nicholas: *The English Physician* (London, 1652).
Dodoens, Rembert: *A Niew Herbal* (1578).
Evelyn, John: *Acetaria*, (1699).
Gerrard, John: *The Herball or Generall Historie of Plants* (John Norton, London, 1597).
Grieves, Mrs M.: *A Modern Herbal* (1931).
Harington, Sir John: *The Englishman's Doctor* (1607).
Holmes, Peter: *The Energetic of Western Herbs* (NatTrop Publishing, Berkeley, USA, 1989).
Hyll, Thomas: *The Proffitable Arte of Gardening* (1568).
Macer, Aemilius: *Of the Virtues of Herbs* (15th century).
Mills, Simon: *Out of the Earth* (Viking Arkana, 1991)
Parkinson, John: *Theatrum Botanicum* (London, 1640).
Pliny: *Natural History* (AD77).
Potts, Billie: *Witches Heal* (Hecuba's Daughters, Inc., 1981).
Ram, William: *Ram's Little Dodoen* (1606).
W.M., Cook to Queen Henrietta Maria: *The Queen's Closet Opened* (1655).

# Useful Addresses

For general information on all aspects of herbs, including growing, medicinal and culinary uses, contact:

UK:   The Herb Society
      PO Box 599, London SW11 4RW

USA:   The Herb Quarterly
      Box 548 MH, Boiling Springs, PA 17007

Australia:   The Australian Herb Society
      PO Box 110
      Mapleton 4560
      Australia

If you need to find a professional medical herbalist for a consultation, the following organizations hold registered lists. To obtain copies of the lists, send an SAE.

UK:   The National Institute of Medical Herbalists
      56 Longbrook Street, Exeter, Devon EX4 6AH

      The General Council and Register of Consultant Herbalists
      18 Sussex Square, Brighton BN2 5AA

USA:   The American Herbalists Guild
      PO Box 1683, Soquel, CA 95073

Australia:   The National Herbalists Association of Australia
      PO Box 65, Kingsgrove, NSW 2208

# Index